Best Dog Hikes
Washington

Best Dog Hikes Washington

Edited by FalconGuides

FALCONGUIDES

GUILFORD, CONNECTICUT

An imprint of Globe Pequot

Falcon and FalconGuides are registered trademarks and Make Adventure Your Story is a trademark of Rowman & Littlefield.

Distributed by NATIONAL BOOK NETWORK

Based on content originally by Natalie Bartley, Allen Cox, Peter Stekel, Oliver Lazerby, Peter Stekel, Roddy Scheer, Adam Sawyer, Jim Yuskavitch, Linda Mullally, David Mullally, Nathan Barnes, and Jeremy Barnes

British Library Cataloguing-in-Publication Information available

Library of Congress Cataloging-in-Publication Data available

ISBN 978-1-4930-2405-6 (paperback)
ISBN 978-1-4930-2406-3 (e-book)

∞™ The paper used in this publication meets the minimum requirements of American National Standard for Information Sciences—Permanence of Paper for Printed Library Materials, ANSI/NISO Z39.48-1992.

Printed in the United States of America

Contents

The Hikes

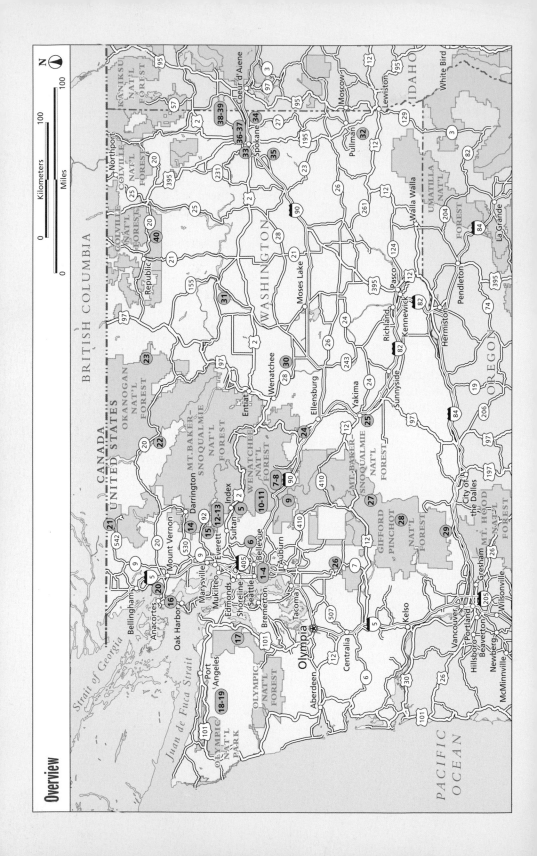

Overview

Introduction

Washington is a hiker's paradise. From the tidal beaches near Seattle to the mountains of the North Cascades and the coulees of central Washington, the state's vast public lands and state and county parks offer enough hiking opportunities to last a lifetime. Add to this the pleasure of sharing these trails with your best friend—i.e., your dog—and you have an activity that will bring you and your pet a significant amount of joy, not to mention healthful exercise. Helping you explore some of Washington's best trails for hiking with a dog is what this book is all about.

Many of Washington's different ecosystems and landscapes are exceptional. The Olympic Peninsula has one of the largest protected landscapes, and the wildest coastline, in the continental United States. The Cascades may not be impressive in elevation alone—much of the range is lower than the lowest point in Colorado—but the state has more than half of all the glaciers in the lower forty-eight. The geology of the eastern, drier side of Washington is dominated by shrub-steppe terrain that was once part of the largest grassland in North America.

Volcanoes are prominent in the current landscape, and they also shaped the flatlands of eastern Washington. Lava flow after lava flow piled up in the Columbia Basin in the Miocene and Pliocene epochs. During the end of the last ice age, some of the largest floods the world has ever seen poured out of Glacial Lake Missoula and carved deep canyons and potholes in the basin. The result left impressive canyons, coulees, and scablands all over the southeastern part of the state and left a path for the present-day Columbia River—another of Washington's natural treasures and one of very few rivers to cut through a major mountain range.

There are a lot of amazing things to see here. The state's beauty is as varied as it is grand. Where else can you ski snowfields in August and surf ocean waves in the same day, explore inland sand dunes one day and ancient forests the next? The staggering variety in terrain can be explored with hikes of all lengths. Often the state's treasures are only a mile from a paved trailhead, or even just outside city limits.

The large protected areas in the Cascades and Olympics make it possible to walk until you're days from the nearest road. The state's mountain ranges are also seemingly at the perfect climate and latitude to be a petri dish for culturing eye-popping scenery. Huge snowfall and mild summers create glaciers. When you see the Cascades or Olympics in summer under a clear blue sky, the white glaciers complete them—a reminder of the long wet winters and improbable elevation of the mountains in our backyard. Flowers bloom just below massive glaciers. Wild coastline, pockets of desert wilderness, and wet and dry slopes offer different terrain and vegetation.

And while Washington is cold and snowy enough for our mountains to be framed by glaciers, summer thaws the mountain soil enough to allow a great variety and number of wildflowers to blossom in every color imaginable. This is a treat that our neighbors to the north don't experience, at least not to the same degree.

If that's not enough, wild mountains are surrounded by ocean and lonely desert. To truly appreciate Washington State's beauty, you must experience the variety. Explore the deserts that are parched and dry thanks to the height of the Cascades. Wander the beaches and gaze offshore, where the storms that blanket our mountains begin.

This book includes hikes that explore the most beautiful places in the state, while also trying to spread them throughout the state's varied terrain. Some hikes in this book are simple strolls just beyond a paved parking lot. Others are long treks to high passes or beyond raging streams. That's the attraction of Washington—beauty and adventure lurk deep in the mountain ranges, but also just beyond city limits.

Weather

Like everything else in the state, the weather is highly variable. The mountains and the west side of the state are overcast and drizzly for most of the year. Luckily, the prime hiking season and the best weather coincide. Summer in Washington can be dry for weeks or even months at a time. In the mountains, though, be prepared for rain even if it's not in the forecast, and expect chilly nighttime temperatures even in summer. Big mountains, and especially the volcanoes, can create their own weather. Most Washington hikers don't leave home without a rain jacket, no matter the season or the forecast.

In general, the closer you are to the coast, the more likely it is to rain. You can use the mountain ranges to your advantage, however. Frequently the weather on the east slopes of the Cascades and Olympics will be much drier than the west slopes. Snow in the Cascades and Olympics melts later than almost anywhere else in the lower forty-eight. Some years you can hike high in the mountains in mid-June; other years you'll encounter snow patches in the high country through August. If you're unsure of the amount of snow in the mountains, call a ranger station. Luckily for Washington residents, the mountains are often visible from far away, and you can get a fairly good idea of how snowy the mountains are just by looking at them.

The snow that ends the hiking season is also fickle. Sometimes the mountains stay summery into October; other years, snow storms blanket the mountains in the beginning of October.

Flora and Fauna

The mighty Douglas fir is everywhere in Western Washington. These trees grow big, especially on the west side of the Olympics. Western red cedar and western hemlock are also common. In the mountains, subalpine fir and mountain hemlock join the Douglas firs. Pine trees march up the east slope of the mountains. Lodgepole, white, and ponderosa pines grow throughout eastern Washington.

Other trees of interest include western larches and quaking aspens. Larches are treasured by Washington hikers. In fall their needles turn a brilliant gold before falling off. The needles are in their prime for one short week, known as "golden week" by

their devotees. Larches are most common on the east slopes of the North Cascades, but they also thrive in the Kettle River Range, and a few spare larches grow in the Selkirk Mountains. Deciduous quaking aspens, which grow in some lowland valleys east of the mountains, also produce brilliant fall colors.

Shrub-steppe desert covers much of southeast Washington. It's a fragile cold-desert ecosystem that's characterized by sagebrush and grasses. Wildflowers are prolific here in spring, including similar species as the alpine meadows but also a host of colorful species unique to these deserts. Washington even has a couple species of native cactus that grow in the shrub-steppe, including hedgehog and prickly pear. There are also some poisonous plants that can be a nuisance for you and your dog (see upcoming section on Seasonal Nuisances).

Anywhere you go in Washington, you'll find deer. Elk roam much of the state as well. Black bears and mountain goats are common in alpine meadows in summer. In recent years, some rare megafauna have shown signs of recovering. The state's first confirmed gray wolf pack appeared in 2008. Today nine wolf packs roam the state, mostly in the northeast corner, with a few in the North and Central Cascades. Moose are also spreading south and west from the northeast, and about fifty grizzly bears currently live in the Washington Selkirks. After a half decade without a confirmed sighting in the North Cascades, a hiker photographed a grizzly bear south of the North Cascades Highway in 2011.

It's important when hiking with your dog to keep in mind the wildlife that might be present in the area. Complete control of your pet is needed. If that means a leash, then use it, because the last thing you want is your dog getting into a fight with a pack of wolves or a bear. Even deer can be dangerous when cornered—more than one dog has been stomped by their hooves. In any case, your dog should absolutely not be chasing deer or any other wildlife.

Parking Passes and Regulations

More than 40 percent of the land in Washington is publicly owned. The majority of that is managed by the USDA Forest Service in the form of national forests or wilderness areas.

To park on forest service land, you'll need to purchase a Northwest Forest Pass, which is good for a year. Washington State has three national parks: North Cascades, Mount Rainier, and Olympic National Parks. For the most part, dogs are not allowed in national parks, although we do include a couple trails in Olympic National Park where dogs are allowed. Some areas in these parks require that you purchase a day pass.

In July 2011 Washington State began requiring an annual Discover Pass to park at state parks, Washington Department of Natural Resources land, and Washington Department of Fish and Wildlife managed land.

Many trailheads in this book require a pass of some sort. Specific information is included in the specs for each hike, along with contact information so you can check with the appropriate government agency for current pricing.

Don't Leave Home without Him

Once you've had the companionship of a dog on the trail, you will never be able to imagine hiking without your canine pal. When it comes to hiking, you and your dog share some benefits in common, but your differences are what enhance and complement your nature experience.

Hiking is an inexpensive opportunity for you and Pooch to stay physically fit and trim while sharing quality time in the absence of all the everyday distractions. The "natural" stimulation of sights, sounds, and smells is a great way for both of you to decompress from the daily urban sensory irritation. You both will be calmer and more relaxed at the end of a day on the trail.

You may be more enthralled than your dog by panoramic vistas, soothed by the gurgling of brooks, excited about the historic significance of the pioneer wagon wheel ruts you see across the trail, or intrigued by the sight of an unusual bird or flowering plant. But the highlight of any dog lover's hike is witnessing the simple euphoric unbridled joy of his or her dog wagging, sniffing, sprinting across a meadow, or bounding into a lake. No trail companion is as enthusiastic about snack breaks as your dog. No trail companion will follow you as faithfully, eagerly, and confidently and express as much gratitude as your dog for taking him on an outdoor adventure.

Unbridled joy on the trail

Getting in Hiking Form

Pups initially receive immunity from their mother's milk, but after they stop nursing they need protection through inoculation. Pups under 4 months old must be protected from infectious disease until they receive all the immunizations recommended by your veterinarian. This is a good time to take your dog outdoors for play and exploring near your home. By 12 weeks and the first of three DHLPP shots, it should be safe to begin socializing with romps with other pups that have been immunized and are current on rabies boosters. This is the ideal time to sign up for a group puppy class that is as much about practicing good manners and redirecting bad habits as it is about social skills.

Start building stamina and confidence in the outside world with daily short (20- to 30-minute) but frequent leash walks in a variety of settings. Begin introducing the pup to sights from the trail like backpacks, hiking sticks, and tents.

It's never too soon to start getting your dog used to car travel, and using a crate will make your pup feel more secure and minimize the risk of sensory overload. Drive the car to nearby parks to build on the positive association of the crate and the car. Done sensibly and sensitively, crate training will produce long-term benefits for both you and your dog.

Four to six months old is the ideal age to venture farther afield to meadows or local trails on leash, but practice recalls at the end of a long rope with treats. Recalls off leash should be done in the house or in a fenced yard and only when you are certain you have your dog's undivided attention. Beginner group obedience classes with a supportive trainer who practices "positive" reinforcement is the best investment you can make in your relationship with your hiking pal.

Never call your dog to you for a reprimand. Why would you run up to someone who calls you over to berate you and make you feel bad about yourself? You want your dog to associate his name being called with fun, pleasant, or tasty experiences.

Your one-on-one training sessions shouldn't last more than 30 minutes, and two 15-minute sessions with a play break in between might get better results if your dog is hyper and has a short attention span.

Do not stress the healthy development of your dog's bones and muscles with over-exertion during the first six months, twelve to eighteen months for large dogs. Stick to flat terrain, and take frequent rest and water stops.

Adult dogs also need to condition their muscles and cardiovascular system if they are new to the sport of hiking. Consult your veterinarian regarding the health and age of your dog. Overweight dogs work harder and overheat faster.

Depending on how sedentary or active your dog has been, getting in shape for the trail can take from a couple of weeks to about a month of consistent twice-daily walking. Sprinting to retrieve a ball in the backyard or on the beach is not the same as a sustained walking pace on a trail for an hour or more.

By now you should have a pretty good sense of your dog's fitness. Use week 5 (see Sample Training Regimen) to maintain his fitness level between hikes. Ideally a dog in his prime (2 to 7 years old) should be going outdoors to exercise, socialize, and get mental stimulation two times a day and get at least 2 hours of physical activity each day. On hot days it is best to exercise early and after sundown. Make sure Pooch has cool fresh water regularly and has access to shade to cool down on hot days.

SAMPLE TRAINING REGIMEN

Weeks 1, 2, and 3—Morning and Evening

15- to 20- minute sniff and stroll (warm-up)

10-minute brisk walk with no pit stops at the fire hydrant (cardiovascular workout)

5-minute sniff and stroll (cooldown)

Week 4—Morning and Evening

15-minute sniff and stroll (warm-up)

30-minute brisk walk (cardiovascular workout)

10-minute sniff and stroll (cooldown)

By week 4 incorporate some hill or stair work, being sure to stop for rest and water breaks.

Week 5—Morning and Evening

15-minute sniff and stroll (warm-up)

30-minute brisk walk (cardiovascular workout)

10-minute sniff and stroll (cooldown)

Week 5 a repeat of week 4, but add one additional longer walk at the end of the week (about 1.5 hours, including some uphill). This longer walk is about distance not speed.

A Word of Caution about Food and Exercise

It is best to feed your dog at least a couple of hours before rigorous exercise and perhaps divide his portion into two smaller portions (half 2 hours prior, the other half 30 minutes after). No one feels good jumping around on a full stomach. Puppies need frequent small feedings throughout the day, and adult dogs should be fed at least two times a day.

Gastric dilatation volvulus (GDV) is commonly known as "bloat" because it causes the stomach to bloat and contort. Running and jumping after a large meal can compound the risks of the stomach twisting in the abdomen (especially in large breeds), blocking the flow or absorption of gastric material. GDV can be fatal. Dividing daily portions into smaller, more frequent meals during rest periods on the trail or in camp can help prevent GDV and is a healthier way to fuel your dog's energy during physical activity.

Pacing and Body Language

Hiking with your dog should not be about forced marches. The whole idea is to get exercise and interact with your dog while your eyes and ears take in your surroundings. This is your best quality bonding time. Savor it. Three miles per hour is a good, steady pace on level terrain at sea level. If you can, time yourself on a local high school track with your dog on leash to get an accurate idea of your pace in ideal conditions. Just remember that on a trail the terrain, weather, and elevation will slow that pace, not to mention your dog's sniff and spray stops, photo ops, and water and snack stops.

Also keep in mind the altitude factor. In the mountains, for every 1,000 feet of elevation gain, you can add an extra mile of walking time. Walking downhill is about three-quarters of the time, not the optimistic half the time most people hope for.

Keep your dog on leash for the first 30 minutes if you are planning to hike more than a couple of miles. Dogs out of the starting gate in a new, natural, stimulating setting can tucker themselves out running in circles. They have no idea about pace.

Watch your dog's body language for tail up and fluid movement to confirm he is feeling strong and happy. Tail down, stiff gait, and lethargy indicate fatigue or injury. When you see this, examine his paws and between the toes for foreign bodies that may be causing discomfort. Stop and rest and offer your dog water and a snack. That might do the trick.

When you head out on the trail, don't forget that you have the distance back to the trailhead to cover, so don't go too far and get stuck having to carry your dog out. If your dog looks drained or demoralized or stops, lies down, or behaves oddly, trust that something is wrong. Dogs have an innate desire to please, and they will go till they blow. There have been instances of dogs dropping dead from exhaustion on a run with their trusted person. Some dogs just don't have body awareness. Some Labs will drown before they stop swimming out for that ball on the 150th throw. Be sensitive and conservative. Shorten the excursion or abort if necessary. Dogs are not machines. Treat your dog as if he were a child dependent on his parent's loving better judgment.

If your dog is on hyper alert, with ears forward, tail up, or raised hackles (hair standing up on the back or neck), his tension and attention might have been triggered by a sound, smell, or sight that you have yet to notice. Put his leash on, look around, and wait a couple of minutes. Proceed cautiously.

If your dog appears jittery, barks, whines, or howls, he may be sensing a potential threat. Pat him and speak to him reassuringly, but respect his concern. Leash him until you identify the source of his concern, which could be as simple as the odd shape of a boulder ahead, another hiker or dog around the bend, or a small critter darting in the bushes.

You want to share safe, positive experiences that will nurture his and your enthusiasm for hiking. Once you have shared the trail with your dog, any other trail companion will seem uninspiring and a dog-less hike will seem humdrum. Hiker dog lovers know that the "high" from hiking begins with having a dog at your side, so prepare wisely, and don't leave home without him!

Gearing Up for Safe Happy Trails

You are solely responsible for your dog's safety and well-being on the trail, as well as his behavior.

There's a hike for every dog (toy, giant, short legged, or fat), but you have to determine the length and pace of your outings by the age, health, physical condition, and breed anatomic characteristics of your dog. While dogs with flatter faces and shorter sinuses—like pugs, for example—are more susceptible to breathing problems exasperated by heat and excessive physical activity, giant breeds like the Bernese mountain dog have bones that grow more slowly, so exercise should be moderate until they reach skeletal maturity, around 2 years old. Annual checkups by your veterinarian help establish the status of your dog's health and what exercise regimen is appropriate to start getting fit for the trail.

Five Building Blocks for Good Trail Dogs

Behind every dog labeled "bad" is usually a naive, oblivious, or irresponsible person with a dazed, glazed, or insouciant look on his or her face.

Bring your dog's favorite toy on the hike.

Good trail etiquette starts with good manners at home. Here are five tips for building the kind of human-dog partnership on the trail that will make hiking with your dog safe and fun, while promoting good "stewardship of the land" so that our public lands can continue to be enjoyed by all:

1. Choose a dog that is compatible with your lifestyle and level of outdoor activity. Some things you need to consider are whether you want a puppy or an adult dog and the breed health history, physical characteristics, temperament, and grooming requirements that you want in a dog. Dogs are social pack animals and are not meant to be isolated at home alone for days on end while you work or play without them. They are not meant to sit in a yard by themselves, even if it does look like the gardens of Versailles. Isolation makes dogs bored, depressed, and sometimes destructive. It is nothing short of cruel. Dogs require time and attention, and the tasks associated with having a dog should be a labor of love rather than laborious obligations.

2. Spaying and neutering your canine companion won't make her fat or make him lazy. It reduces risks of mammary gland and prostate cancers. It saves them from being slaves to the hormonal drive to reproduce. He won't be obsessed with roaming, and she won't be scratching her address on fire hydrants. It will make them focus on you and their obedience training homework and make them more congenial with other dogs on the trail.

3. Good manners matter. The only answer to your doubts about your dog's good behavior and responsiveness to your voice commands is a leash. No wildlife should be stressed by a run-amok dog, and no one likes to be rushed by an over-exuberant dog. Some people fear dogs, and others dislike them—to put it mildly. The easiest solution for park authorities and business owners who receive complaints is to ban dogs from trails, restaurants, and hotels.

   Being off leash is fun, and teaching your dog basic commands like sit, stay, and come is his ticket to the mother of all privileges: off-leash playtime. A well-trained dog is appreciated by fellow hikers and others who share the trail, not to mention that responsiveness to voice commands could someday save your dog's life. Signing up for positive-training obedience classes early on is an investment in your and your dog's relationship that you will never regret. If the only skill your dog learns is to walk at the end of a leash without strangling himself and pulling you off your feet, it will make strolling the neighborhood and the trail a joyful experience rather than a dreaded exercise in frustration.

4. Socialize your dog around strangers and strange things to prevent "overreaction" past the "imprint" stage in the tenth to twelfth week of life. Trash cans on the street corner should not be perceived as a threat, and neither should boulders on the side of the trail. Pack animals coming up the trail should not unglue your dog. Expose your dog to trail sights as early as possible. Pups should have had their series of vaccinations before venturing out, but who says you can't walk around the yard with a backpack and hiking sticks? Get your dog used

Carefully crossing a stream

to objects that move, like bicycles and cars, so he doesn't develop phobias that can trigger neurotic episodes that can endanger him, you, and others on the trail. Introduce your dog to water. Dogs don't have to like dipping in streams and swimming in lakes, but they should learn to walk near and across water without panicking. It requires time and sensitivity on your part.

5. Before hitting the trail, consult your veterinarian about required vaccinations, booster shots (rabies), and the most current preventives for ticks and Lyme disease, mosquitoes, and heartworm. Also ask about the safest flea and tick products.

Pooch Essentials and Trail Readiness

The following will get your dog started on a safe paw.

The Essentials

1. Choose a harness. Hands down, harnesses are safer than collars. Dogs don't accidentally choke on harnesses. Harnesses make crossing streams and negotiating passages along precarious stretches of trail much safer. Harnesses allow for a quicker, safer, and solid grab of your dog if necessary. If you don't use a harness, **never** let your dog run around off leash with a choke chain–type collar.
2. Lead your dog with a 6-foot leather or nylon leash. Retractable leashes are an invitation to chaos when passing people with dogs who like to do the

ring-around-the-rosy sniff-and-greet dance on the trail. Leather leashes last forever, but colorful nylon leashes can be easily located and dry quickly when wet.

3. Have your dog wear an identification tag. Tattooing and microchipping your dog are a great idea and work better in urban areas. But on the trail, an old-fashioned tag with your dog's name and your cell phone number is much more likely to reunite you with wayward Fido. Always attach a temporary tag with the name of your campground, cabin resort, or whatever lodging you are using as a base camp on your adventure. Some dog-friendly accommodations include a temporary tag with the business's name and phone number and your room or cabin number.

4. Bring biodegradable dog waste bags for pack-it-in, pack-it-out trails and campground areas.

5. Get your dog used to wearing booties. Hiking dogs should learn to be comfortable wearing booties in the event they are needed on the trail. Fit your dog with booties, and let him get used to them in the house and on your neighborhood walks. Always have a set of booties in your or his pack for the unexpected tender tootsies on paw-bruising trails.

6. Pack water and energy-boosting snacks. Never count on finding water on the trail. Instead, carry 8 ounces of water for every hour or 2.0 miles of trail. Heat + Altitude + Exertion = Dehydration, which is the most common and preventable hiking hazard for both you and your dog.

7. Trim your dog's nails and cut dewclaws short to prevent snags that can tear the tissue.

8. Groom your long- or curly-coated dog for summer hiking for his comfort and your sanity. Choose function over fashion so that his coat doesn't sweep up and trap burrs, foxtails, and dirt debris and turn your hike into a grooming nightmare.

9. Keep your dog's vaccinations current and carry proof of rabies vaccine in his pack; you may be asked for this at some park entrances.

10. Carry a basic first-aid kit (see Appendix B).

Shopping for booties

Pack fitting

Dog Packs

There are several benefits to proper pack training. Some dogs are serious workaholics, and walking along the stream just to smell the wild roses just doesn't cut it. A sense of mission and purpose brings the best out of some of the more hyperactive dogs, while channeling the energies and focus of the smart and free-spirited ones. Carrying some of the load just makes the cut-loose romping time breaks that much more meaningful and ecstatic. The pack should be in proportion to your dog's build and height. It should fit his chest and shoulder contours comfortably without chafing and should be balanced. Dogs should never carry more than one-fourth of their own weight.

To get your dog ready to carry a pack, let him get used to the weight of an empty pack. Use treats to reinforce the association of the pack with something pleasant. Let your dog wear the pack on his daily walks. Gradually stuff the pack with paper, face-cloths, treats, kibble, and dog waste bags. Increase the balanced load over a couple of weeks in preparation for trail day. Take frequent snack breaks on the trail, and remove the pack during each break.

What to Expect on the Trail

Knowledge and information can make your excursions more positive and fun experiences for you and your dog, as they help prepare you for wildlife encounters, seasonal nuisances, other trail users, and Mother Nature's changing moods.

Plan Ahead

Always confirm ahead of time that dogs are welcome on the trail you plan to hike. Policies change, so call the managing agency about any restrictions and abide by the rules.

The managing agency or ranger district office can answer questions about permits, weather (critical information for the high country, where changes can be sudden and extreme even in summer), road closures, trail damage and changes, campground availability, and special advisories. Budget cuts reduce resources and manpower, which impact trail maintenance and campground operation. Visitor centers often depend on volunteers. National forest headquarters have recreation managers and some national forests have "district" recreation managers, who are typically the most informed. To get the most up-to-date information—especially early in the season—it is important to speak to someone who has recently hiked the trail and traveled the roads to the trailhead.

Know Where You Are

Carry relevant maps and know how to read a topographic map so you can study the terrain in the area of your hike and anticipate elevation changes, difficulty, shady spots, water sources, and suitability for your dog. It will help you pack and pace yourself (for every 1,000 feet of elevation, add about an extra mile of time).

USGS quad maps with a scale of 1:24,000 and a compass are the traditional means of navigation. USGS maps do not show road or trail changes that have occurred since their publication, but the USGS is in the process of updating and digitalizing the "legacy" maps (www.USGS.gov/3DEP). Using a compass with a map requires some study and practice. Consider signing up for a navigation workshop at a local outdoor recreation store like R.E.I. or a local community college.

A good GPS (Global Positioning System) unit and maybe even a smartphone with a good mapping app should enable you to determine your approximate location along the trail. Usually, a GPS more accurately shows latitude and longitude but is less accurate at showing elevation. Electronic devices have their limits. Reception of any electronic device depends on receiving correct signals from satellites or cell towers. Remember to fully charge your devices and carry spare batteries. However, even if you are a techno-savvy hiker, it is wise to also carry a map and compass—and know how to use them.

Other Trail Users and Etiquette

On some hikes you will share the trail with people on horseback going out for a trail ride or on a backcountry trek with pack animals in tow. Mountain bikers may also be on some trails. And you will most definitely meet other hikers with or without dogs on and off leash.

Good trail etiquette breeds goodwill and positive relations with other trail users, especially those who may not be fans of dogs on the trail. Here are some general tips:
1. On or off leash, on the trail or in the campground, your dog must be under control.

Yielding to other trail users

2. Friendly exuberance or not, never let your dog charge or bark at other dogs, hikers, or horses. Some people are afraid of dogs. Dogs can also spook horses and jeopardize the safety of the rider. Always step off the trail to the upper side so the horse(s) can see you, keep a tight leash on your dog, and command him to sit until the riders have gone by.
3. Hike only where dogs are permitted, and abide by the posted regulations.
4. Stay on the trail, step lightly in pristine wilderness areas, and don't let your dog chase wildlife.
5. Pack out everything you pack in. At the very least bury your dog's scat away from the trail and surface water. Better yet: Carry it out in biodegradable poop-scoop bags. Dog doo on trails is the number-one complaint by responsible dog owners as well as non–dog owners. It's disgusting and inconsiderate to humans, and it's a territory marker/intruder alert that can stress resident wildlife.
6. Camp in designated campsites in heavily used or developed areas. Never leave your dog unattended in the campground.

Dogs That Want to Rumble

At one time or another, your dog may be a partner in a dominance dance with another dog. This occurs more frequently between males, especially intact males that reek of testosterone. Dogs well versed in pack hierarchy know to stay out of an alpha dog's face or to assume the subordinate body language that stops the music.

To help avoid problems, neuter your male dog before 1 year of age or as soon as both testicles drop. Overt dominance may not appear until he is 2 years old. Neutering reduces macho and roaming instincts. Be aware that testosterone levels take several months to decrease after neutering. Spay your female. Breeding females can be instinctively more competitive around other females. A female in season should never be on the trail. She will create havoc, and her mating instincts will override her flawless obedience record every time.

A leashed dog can be overly protective. Avoid stress by taking a detour around other hikers with dogs or stepping off the trail with your dog at a sit while the other hiker and dog walk by. Do not panic at the hint of raised hackles and loud talk. Most of it is just posturing. If your dog is off leash, stay calm and keep walking away from the other dog while encouraging your dog to come in your most enthusiastic voice and with the promise of a biscuit. If she complies, reward her with a "good dog" and the promised biscuit for positive reinforcement.

Walking back toward the dogs, screaming, and interfering before they resolve their conflict can stoke the fires of a more serious brawl. If the squabble escalates into a dogfight, make sure you cover your arms and hands before trying to break it up. Pull the dogs by the tail, lift their hind legs off the ground, or throw water on them to distract them. As a last resort you may have to throw sand or dirt in the eyes of the one with the grip. One hiker, who uses a cane as a hiking stick, reports having broken up a dogfight or two by slipping the crook of his cane under the dog collar or harness to drag the aggressor away.

To help avoid dogfights, do not give treats to other hikers' dogs. Competition for food and protection of territory are the root of most dogfights.

Seasonal Nuisances
Foxtails
These arrow-like grasses are at their worst in late summer and early fall, when they are dry, sharp, and just waiting to burrow into some dog's fuzzy coat. A dry foxtail can be inhaled by a dog, lodge itself in the ear canal or between the toes, or camouflage itself in the dog's undercoat, puncturing the skin and causing infection. Foxtails have the potential to cause damage to vital organs.

Inspect your dog's ears and toes, and run your hands through his coat, inspecting under the belly, legs, and tail. Brush out his coat after excursions where there were even hints of foxtails. Violent sneezing and snorting is an indication he may have inhaled a foxtail. Even if the sneezing or shaking decreases in intensity or frequency, the foxtail can still be tucked where it irritates only occasionally while it travels deeper, causing more serious damage. If this happens, take your dog to a vet as soon as possible. He may have to be anesthetized to remove the foxtail.

Poison Oak
Poison oak is a three-leaved, low-growing vine or bush that ranges in color from green to red depending on the season. The plant can cause topical irritations on hairless areas of your dog's body. (You can apply cortisone cream to the affected area.)

Find out if there is poison oak where you plan to hike, and make sure you wash your hands with soap after handling your dog. The irritating oil (urushiol) can rub off your dog onto you, your sleeping bag, your car seat, and your furniture at home. If you are very sensitive to urushiol, bathe your dog after the hike and sponge your arms and legs with diluted chlorine bleach, Tecnu soap, or anti-itch spray. Tecnu soap is an outdoor cleanser that removes plant oil from your skin and also can be used on your laundry.

Other Poisonous Plants

Unfortunately, your dog may be tempted to taste and chew hazardous plants. This includes plants found in your backyard, like rhubarb. In the wilderness there are similar dangers—plants such as rhododendrons may cause considerable sickness and discomfort for your pet.

If you suspect poisoning, take note of what your dog ate and head back to the car. Once out of the woods, call your vet or the ASPCA National Animal Poison Control Center (888-426-4435).

Fleas and Ticks

Fleas are uncomfortable for your dog and carry tapeworm eggs, and ticks are one of nature's most painfully potent and tenacious creatures for their size. Some tick bites cause uncomfortable red, swollen irritation to the area of the skin where they attach and can make the area feel like it was pounded by a two-by-four. In some cases, tick bites can inflict temporary paralysis. Other types of ticks found in Washington can carry Lyme disease, which is reported to be the most common tick-borne disease in the United States.

Ticks thrive on wild hosts (deer are the most common) around lakes, streams, meadows, and some wooded areas. They cling to unsuspecting hikers and dogs. On dogs they crawl out of the fur and attach to the skin around the neck, face, ears, stomach, or any soft, fleshy cavity. They attach to their hosts by sticking their mouthparts into the skin and then feed on the host's blood and swell up until they dangle from the skin like an ornament.

REMOVING A TICK

- Try not to break off any mouthparts (remaining parts can cause infection), and avoid getting tick fluids on you through crushing or puncturing the tick.
- Grasp the tick as close to the skin as possible with blunt forceps or tweezers or with your fingers in rubber gloves, tissue, or any barrier to shield your skin from possible tick fluids.
- Remove the tick with a steady pull.
- After removing the tick, disinfect the skin with alcohol and wash your hands with soap and water.

There is an abundance of chemical and natural flea and tick products on the market, including collars, dips, sprays, powders, pills, and oils. Some products have the advantages of being effective on both fleas and ticks, remain effective on wet dogs, and require an easy once-a-month topical application. Consult your veterinarian about a safe and appropriate product.

Mosquitoes

Avon's Skin-So-Soft is a less toxic and more pleasant-smelling—though not nearly as effective—mosquito repellent than products containing DEET. Mix one cap of the oil with one pint of water in a spray bottle. Spray your dog and run your hands through her coat from head to toe and tail to cover her with a light film of the mixture. Be careful to avoid her eyes and nostrils, but do not miss the outer ear areas. Organic solutions containing eucalyptus can also be used as a mosquito repellent. Besides being annoying, mosquitoes carry heartworm. Consult your veterinarian about preventive medication.

Bees, Wasps, Hornets, and Yellow Jackets

These insects' nests can be in trees or on the ground.

Moody Mother Nature and Seasonal Hazards

Every season has climatic constants, but Mother Nature can be temperamental, bringing additional unexpected challenges that can affect your safety and the safety of your dog.

Stopping for a water break on the trail

Summer

Heat can be taxing on your dog. While western Washington temperatures are usually moderated by the Pacific Ocean, central and eastern Washington can get quite hot in summer, which increases the risks of dehydration and heatstroke. Here are some tips to help avoid heat-related trouble:

- Hike in the early morning or late afternoon.
- Carry at least 8 ounces of water per dog for each hour on the trail or 2.0 miles of trail. Identify water sources near the trail in advance of your hike, and plan for a lack thereof if necessary.
- Rest in a shaded area during the intensity of midday.
- Take frequent rest stops and offer your dog water.
- Let your dog take a plunge in a lake or lie belly down in a stream or mud puddle to cool down.

Winter

Winter-like conditions can affect your dog's feet, endurance, and body warmth. Crusty snow can chafe and cut your dog's pads, and walking in deep snow is very taxing and can put a short-haired dog at risk of hypothermia. Here are some ways to protect your dog from cold and extra exertion.

- Carry booties for icy conditions and use them on your dog if she is not accustomed to snow and ice. Even dogs accustomed to snow can get abraded paws. Check your pup's feet for chafing, and carry a couple extra booties as replacements for any lost in the snow. Keeping your dog on leash while she is in booties makes it easier to know when to adjust them or to retrieve any that slip off.
- Clothing on dogs should be about function, not fashion. Consider a wool or polypropylene sweater for your short-haired dog or down if your dog has no undercoat.
- Encourage your dog to walk behind you in your tracks. It is less strenuous.
- Carry a small sled or snow disk with an insulated foam pad so your dog can rest off the frozen ground.
- Unless your dog is a northern breed that thrives in cold, keep your outings shorter in transition seasons when there is some snow and ice to navigate. Carry snacks like liver or jerky treats and warm drinking water.
- Winter in much of Washington is hike friendly at lower elevations, though it can bring heavy rain. However, winter conditions in the mountains can be extreme, even life threatening, to hikers and their furry companions. Check the weather forecast, and be prepared for potential problems to your dog's comfort on the trail.

Spring

Following the cooler winter months, spring brings warmer temperatures and beautiful wildflowers to Washington, but it can still be quite rainy. High snowy passes usually don't melt until midsummer, and creeks swollen with meltwater can be treacherous, so exercise caution and make sure you have proper equipment for the conditions. Be prepared for ticks, mosquitoes, cheatgrass, stinging nettles, poison oak, and foxtails that are coming to life after the cold winter.

Fall

Fall brings shorter daylight hours. Adjust the length of your hikes accordingly. Hunting season in many parts of the backcountry requires extra caution. Check the hunting regulations and dates for the hiking area you have in mind. It is important that you and your dog wear bright colors when hiking anywhere in the fall. Orange hunting vests are available for dogs; colorful harnesses and bandannas are also a good idea. When in doubt about hunting in forested areas, keep your dog on a leash.

The High Country

The high country is subject to variable and extreme weather year-round. Check for weather advisories at the ranger station, including thunderstorm warnings and fire danger. Afternoon thunderstorms are common in the high country. Rain can quickly turn to hail and snow. Stay below the timberline and off exposed ridges. In spring and fall pay attention to sudden drops in temperature and shifts in wind, with system clouds announcing snowfall.

Taking a break overlooking a lake

How to Use This Guide

While this book is called *Best Dog Hikes Washington*, the fact is that the hikes included are most certainly *not* the only hikes suitable to hiking with your dog. On the contrary. In some regions of Washington there is such an abundance of fabulous trails that the biggest hurdle was deciding which ones to include. Although there are a few moderately challenging mountain-peak hikes included, this book is not about conquering any summits with crampons on your feet and a dog on your back. The goal is to introduce you and your dog to trails of various lengths and difficulty that showcase the best attributes likely to excite you and your dog and inspire you to explore the region and discover other hikes that could become your and your dog's favorites.

We chose hikes of various distances and terrain to satisfy the younger or more eager dog that already has some trail dust under his paws as well as the older, less-ambitious or novice dog on his first foray out of the burbs. It is up to you to build up your dog's fitness with regular consistent exercise and to monitor his body language for signs of discomfort, pain, or fatigue. Don't risk injuring your dog by making him a weekend warrior.

Distances were calculated using USGS, forest, wilderness, and area-specific maps in tandem with a GPS unit for maximum accuracy. Be aware that it is not uncommon for trails to be rerouted from their original USGS mapping as a result of floods, fires, and slides or changes in agency policy.

Hikes are divided into three categories: easy, moderate, and strenuous. A short hike may be more strenuous than a longer one because of elevation gain. Hikes under 5.0 miles will always mention if there are characteristics that would make the otherwise easy or moderate hike strenuous. The assumption in determining the degree of difficulty is that you and your dog have driven from sea level or low elevation to the trailhead, so hikes with elevations of 5,000 feet and above are labeled moderate at best or strenuous. You must exercise some personal judgment as to the suitability of a hike based on your and your dog's general fitness levels.

The bolded specs below each hike overview is an outline to assist you in preparing for the hike. It includes the following features.

Distance is the total roundtrip distance of the hike, with a notation on whether the hike is an out-and-back, loop, or lollipop.

Hiking time is based on a 2.0-mile-per-hour pace, taking into account water and snack breaks, Pooch swim stops, and vista points. Hikers' pace will vary according to individual fitness levels, pack weight, terrain, and elevation range, especially if the hikes begin above 5,000 feet. When hiking uphill, add 1.0 mile or 30 minutes for every 1,000 feet gained in elevation. One way to estimate your average pace per mile on level ground for a baseline is to time yourself walking around a running track.

Difficulty rates hikes as easy, moderate, or difficult.

Trail surface indicates what you'll be walking on, which is especially important for dogs' paws. If a trail has a lot of rock or a surface that could be especially abrasive to dogs' paws on extended stretches, we will note booties should be worn.

Best season to hike a trail is determined by the trail's accessibility during different times of the year, which depends on the regional weather. Too much snow or rain during certain months can make a trail hard to navigate. Spring can last anywhere from early April to late May or mid-June. Summer is typically late June through August. Fall can begin in early September and last into November. Winter begins to show its teeth in December and lasts through March.

Note that the opening dates of trails and campgrounds, especially in the Cascades, are subject to the length and intensity of the winter season, and that can vary by several weeks from year to year. Optimally the season runs from Memorial Day weekend to mid-October, but don't count on it. Trails in the high country frequently still have snow after Independence Day. Although the trail may be accessible year-round, "Best season" will list the preferable months or seasons for optimal enjoyment and comfort, influenced by temperature, trail traffic, water sources, seasonal highlights like wildflowers and fall foliage, as well as nuisances like excessive mosquitoes and poison oak. Always call the ranger station for trail status.

Other trail users lets you know if you and your pooch will be sharing the trail with horses, which include pack animals, and/or bikes. Those are the two most common trail users and require dogs to be on exemplary behavior or, better yet, on a leash.

Canine compatibility will indicate if a leash is required. Different land management agencies have different policies regarding leashes versus voice control. Always check at the trailhead; this information is usually available there. If you don't have absolute voice control of your dog when hiking, then a leash is almost always a good idea. In general, dogs are allowed under voice control in wilderness areas and on national forest lands. However, they do need to be leashed on these lands when in or around developed recreation sites, trailheads, interpretive trails, or campgrounds. It's also recommended that you keep your dog on a leash whenever you are hiking near overlooks, steep drop-offs, caves, swift runoff rivers, or anywhere else that may present a danger to your dog.

Fees and permits applies to parking, day hiking, or overnight camping fees.

Schedule will tell you if a certain trail system has any opening or closing times.

Maps refers you to the appropriate USGS topographical map and/or national forest, wilderness, or additional park or local maps. (Be sure to check the "contour interval" when using USGS maps. Although most are 40 feet, some are 20, 25, or 80 feet, and some are in meters.)

Trail contact leads you to the best source for information on permits, fees, dog policies, parking, and campgrounds, as well as current information on access to trails, restrictions, and closures. There is no such thing as asking too many questions when it involves your and your dog's safety. Never drive past a ranger station without taking the opportunity to verify your information.

The Snoqualmie River (Hike 6) © ISTOCK.COM/GMC3101

Special considerations includes a variety of other useful information you may want, depending on the specific hike.

Finding the trailhead gives you driving directions to the trailhead from a significant population base or community located along the principal highway route.

The Hike describes the history and other interesting factoids related to the area of the trail, as well as a description of some of the natural or cultural highlights along the trail.

Miles and Directions gets you from the trailhead to the turnaround point with concise directions between waypoints at trail junctions and significant points of interest.

Map Legend

Municipal

≡⟨90⟩≡ Interstate Highway

≡⟨101⟩≡ US Highway

≡⟨20⟩≡ State Road

≡⟨4934⟩≡ Local/Forest Road

═ ═ ═ ═ Unpaved Road

├──┼──┤ Railroad

─ ─ · ─ State Border

Trails

▬ ▬ ▬ Featured Trail

─ ─ ─ ─ Trail

· · · · · · Off-Route Hike

Water Features

Body of Water

Glacier

Marsh

River/Creek

Intermittent Stream

Waterfall

Rapids

Spring

Symbols

🛏 Bench

Boat Ramp

≍ Bridge

■ Building/Point of Interest

Δ Campground

¡ Gate

🅿 Parking

≍ Pass

▲ Peak/Elevation

🎪 Picnic Area

•─•─• Power Line

Ranger Station/Park Office

Restroom

Scenic View

① Tower/Lookout

Town

○ Trailhead

? Welcome Center

Land Management

National Park/Forest

National Wilderness

State/County Park

Trail Finder

Easy Hikes

1. Seward Park Loop
2. Arboretum Waterfront Trail
3. Burke-Gilman Trail: Gas Works Park to Fremont
4. Magnuson Park
6. Preston-Snoqualmie Trail: Lake Alice to Snoqualmie Falls Overlook
9. Mirror Lake
15. Robe Canyon Historic Park–Lime Kiln Trail
18. Spruce Railroad Trail
19. Madison Creek Falls
25. Cowiche Canyon
29. Lewis River
30. Ancient Lakes
32. Kamiak Butte Pine Ridge Trail
35. Columbia Plateau Trail
36. Iller Creek Conservation Area
37. Centennial Trail
38. Entrance Loop

Moderate Hikes

7. Snow Lake
10. Taylor River
13. Lake Twenty-two
14. Boulder River–Feature Show Falls
16. Deception Pass State Park–Goose Rock
20. Oyster Dome
22. Maple Pass Loop
23. Tiffany Mountain
24. Manastash Ridge–Ray Westberg Trail
26. Pack Forest
31. Northrup Canyon
33. Bowl and Pitcher Loop
34. Liberty Creek–Camp Hughes Loop
40. Sherman Peak Loop

Difficult Hikes

5. Lake Serene
8. Lake Lillian
11. Kendall Katwalk
12. Gothic Basin
17. Marmot Pass
21. Yellow Aster Butte
27. Snowgrass Flat
28. Dog Mountain Loop
39. Mount Kit Carson–Day Mountain Loop

Less than 5 Miles

1. Seward Park Loop
2. Arboretum Waterfront Trail
3. Burke-Gilman Trail: Gas Works Park to Fremont
4. Magnuson Park
6. Preston-Snoqualmie Trail: Lake Alice to Snoqualmie Falls Overlook
9. Mirror Lake
14. Boulder River–Feature Show Falls
18. Spruce Railroad Trail
19. Madison Creek Falls
23. Tiffany Mountain
24. Manastash Ridge–Ray Westberg Trail
30. Ancient Lakes
32. Kamiak Butte Pine Ridge Trail
38. Entrance Loop

5 to 10 Miles

5. Lake Serene
7. Snow Lake
8. Lake Lillian
10. Taylor River
12. Gothic Basin
13. Lake Twenty-two
15. Robe Canyon Historic Park–Lime Kiln Trail
16. Deception Pass State Park–Goose Rock
20. Oyster Dome
21. Yellow Aster Butte
22. Maple Pass Loop
25. Cowiche Canyon

26. Pack Forest
27. Snowgrass Flat
28. Dog Mountain Loop
29. Lewis River
31. Northrup Canyon
33. Bowl and Pitcher Loop
34. Liberty Creek–Camp Hughes Loop
35. Columbia Plateau Trail
36. Iller Creek Conservation Area
37. Centennial Trail
40. Sherman Peak Loop

More than 10 Miles
11. Kendall Katwalk
17. Marmot Pass
39. Mount Kit Carson–Day Mountain Loop

On-Leash Hikes
1. Seward Park Loop
2. Arboretum Waterfront Trail
3. Burke-Gilman Trail: Gas Works Park to Fremont
4. Magnuson Park (large off-leash area nearby)
6. Preston-Snoqualmie Trail: Lake Alice to Snoqualmie Falls Overlook
16. Deception Pass State Park–Goose Rock
18. Spruce Railroad Trail
19. Madison Creek Falls
20. Oyster Dome
24. Manastash Ridge–Ray Westberg Trail
25. Cowiche Canyon
28. Dog Mountain Loop
30. Ancient Lakes
31. Northrup Canyon
32. Kamiak Butte Pine Ridge Trail
33. Bowl and Pitcher Loop
34. Liberty Creek–Camp Hughes Loop
35. Columbia Plateau Trail
36. Iller Creek Conservation Area
37. Centennial Trail
38. Entrance Loop

Voice Control Hikes

5. Lake Serene
7. Snow Lake
8. Lake Lillian
9. Mirror Lake
10. Taylor River
11. Kendall Katwalk
12. Gothic Basin
13. Lake Twenty-two
14. Boulder River–Feature Show Falls
17. Marmot Pass
21. Yellow Aster Butte
22. Maple Pass Loop
23. Tiffany Mountain
26. Pack Forest
27. Snowgrass Flat
29. Lewis River
40. Sherman Peak Loop

Enjoying a waterfall at Big Creek Bridge (Hike 10) PETER STEKEL

1 Seward Park Loop

Seward Park juts into Lake Washington like a thumb. Seattle city officials had the foresight to acquire the wild, wooded property in 1892 and eventually turn it into the public space we enjoy today. The loop trail circles the park on a closed-off service road for most of its length, with the lake on one side and Seattle's largest remaining old-growth forest on the other.

Distance: 2.4-mile loop
Hiking time: About 1 hour
Difficulty: Easy, flat trail
Trail surface: Paved
Best season: Year-round
Other trail users: Bicyclists, skaters
Canine compatibility: Leashed dogs permitted

Fees and permits: No fees or permits required
Schedule: Open daily, 6 a.m. to 10 p.m.
Maps: USGS Seattle South E, Bellevue South W; Seattle street map
Trail contact: Seattle Parks and Recreation; (206) 684-4075; www.seattle.gov/parks
Special considerations: None

Finding the trailhead: From I-5 take exit 163 (South Columbian Way). Follow South Columbian Way to Beacon Avenue South and turn right. Take the first left onto Orcas Avenue South and follow it until it becomes Lake Washington Boulevard South and, curving right, ends in Seward Park. The trailhead is beside the Art Studio building. GPS: N47 33.11' / W122 15.42'

The Hike

Lake Washington—a 20-mile-long lake lined with waterfront homes and parks—defines Seattle's eastern boundary. One of the city's most beautiful parks, Seward Park occupies Bailey Peninsula and is home to an environmental and Audubon center, a clay art studio, an amphitheater, picnic facilities, and miles of trails. The longest and most scenic of the park's trails is the Seward Park Loop (trail #10 on the park's official map, available on their website). This wide, paved trail doubles as a service road that is closed to motorized public traffic.

The trailhead for this hike is at the edge of the lake near the art studio. As you skirt the perimeter of the peninsula, it's easy to forget that you're still connected to the mainland. The setting has the distinctive feel of an island. In fact, Seward Park once was an island; it became attached to the mainland when the building of the locks on the ship canal lowered Lake Washington's water level.

The trail leads to a fishing pier and a wide swimming beach and lawn before rounding North Beach at the tip of the peninsula. Here Mercer Island, with its luxury waterfront homes and forested hillside neighborhoods, comes into full view.

The trail narrows from a service road to a wide footpath in its ending stretch. If it's a clear day—or at least one with a high enough cloud cover—you will be rewarded with an unobstructed view of massive Mount Rainier dominating the horizon about 70 miles to the south.

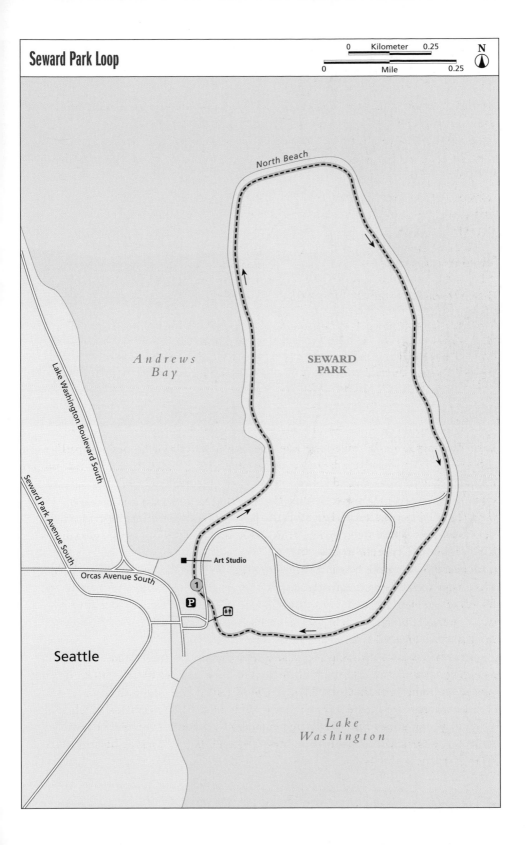

Seward Park Loop

0 — Kilometer — 0.25

0 — Mile — 0.25

N

North Beach

Andrews Bay

SEWARD PARK

Lake Washington Boulevard South

Seward Park Avenue South

Orcas Avenue South

Art Studio

1

P

Seattle

Lake Washington

Mount Rainier from Seward Park © ISTOCK.COM/GMC3101

Miles and Directions

0.0 Start at the trailhead next to the Seward Park Art Studio for a clockwise loop. *Option:* To follow the loop counterclockwise, start at the parking lot at the end of Lake Washington Boulevard South.

0.7 Pass a fishing pier and swimming beach.

1.7 The trail narrows to a footpath.

2.4 Arrive back at the art studio trailhead.

2 Arboretum Waterfront Trail

A ship canal slices Seattle in half, connecting Puget Sound to Lake Washington. At the lake end of the canal, the Arboretum Waterfront Trail follows the marshy shoreline across two islands with views across Union Bay to the University of Washington and Husky Stadium. It is part of a larger network of trails through the 230-acre Washington Park Arboretum and offers an up-close glimpse of marshland flora and fauna, making this easy trail a hit with wildlife photographers.

Distance: 0.9 mile out and back
Hiking time: About 30 minutes
Difficulty: Easy, flat trail
Trail surface: Soil, bark, concrete and metal grate footbridges
Best season: Year-round
Other trail users: None
Canine compatibility: Leashed dogs permitted

Fees and permits: No fees or permits required
Schedule: Open daily from dawn to dusk
Maps: USGS Seattle North E; Seattle street map
Trail contact: Washington Park Arboretum, University of Washington; (206) 543-8800; www.depts.washington.edu/wpa
Special considerations: None

Finding the trailhead: From I-5 take exit 168 and merge onto WA 520 East. Take the first exit (Montlake Boulevard). Immediately across Montlake Boulevard, make a slight right at Lake Washington Boulevard East and turn left at 24th Avenue East. Follow the signs to McCurdy Park and the Museum of History and Industry (MOHAI). Park in the lower lot behind the museum and look for a trailhead kiosk near the lakeshore. GPS: N47 38.75' / W122 17.98'

The Hike

For many Seattleites, the Arboretum Waterfront Trail is a favorite. Its short length offers a quick, accessible break from city life. Footbridges carry a sizable length of the route over the water, giving the trail a unique character. Views of the university, passing boat traffic, and the abundant waterfowl that make the marshes their home give hikers plenty to look at; binoculars or a camera with a zoom lens comes in handy on this hike.

Begin the trail at the kiosk at the water's edge behind the Museum of History and Industry. The kiosk displays an excellent map of the trail. Follow the trail to the right. Almost immediately, the trail crosses a footbridge to Marsh Island, where the raised bark-covered trail keeps your boots dry as it cuts through low, marshland woods and along the lakeshore. A few short spur trails lead to tucked-away concrete floats that are great spots for hikers to stop and view the lake activity as well as docking spots for kayakers and canoers.

As you hike this trail, you may be aware of the rush of traffic on nearby WA 520 as it flows onto the Evergreen Point Floating Bridge. The traffic doesn't seem to deter hikers, as evidenced by the trail's heavy use.

Arboretum Waterfront Trail

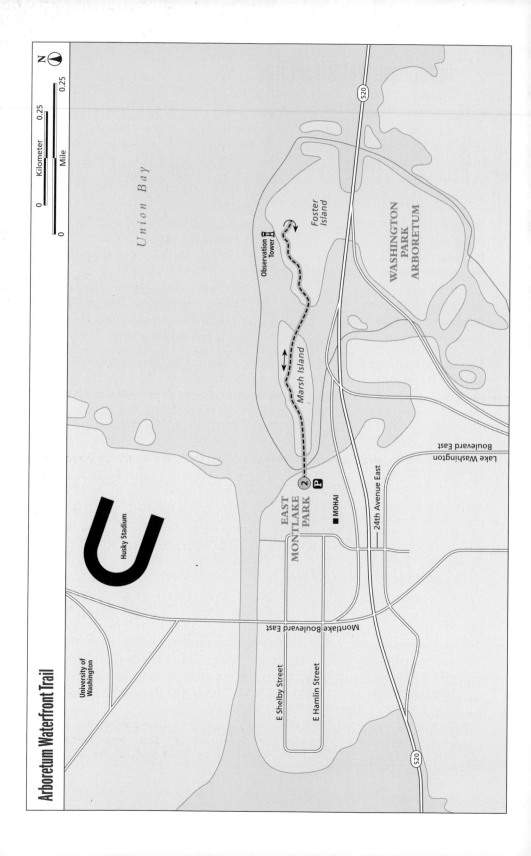

Interesting signposts along the Arboretum Waterfront Trail © ISTOCK.COM/SEASTOCK

The trail leads across a bridge from Marsh Island to Foster Island. On Foster much of the trail is built on a network of bridges that lead you away from shore for a duck's-eye view of the marshy shoreline. This is one of the most interesting features of the trail and is a great place to spot a variety of waterfowl. After the bridge, a short spur trail leads to a raised viewing platform that offers superb views of the ship canal, Lake Washington, the University of Washington, and the waterfront homes of the Laurelhurst district across Union Bay.

Continuing on the main trail for a short distance brings you to the end of the Arboretum Waterfront Trail and the beginning of the trail that leads farther into the arboretum. Turn around at this point and retrace your steps to the trailhead, or continue on for a further exploration of the 230-acre park.

Miles and Directions

0.0 Start at the kiosk near the lakeshore. Facing the kiosk, the trail leads to the left or the right. Follow the trail to the right.

0.45 Reach a kiosk where the trail leaves the marsh and enters an open grassy area. Turn around here and retrace your steps. **Option:** For an extended hike, continue following this trail to the right to reach a larger network of Washington Park Arboretum trails.

0.9 Arrive back at the trailhead kiosk.

3 Burke-Gilman Trail: Gas Works Park to Fremont

The Burke-Gilman Trail is a heavily traveled multiuse recreational corridor that follows an early railroad route. The entire trail runs more than 18 miles and is part of an extensive network of trails in the region. The portion of the Burke-Gilman Trail between Gas Works Park and Fremont, near the trail's southwest end, offers a glimpse of Seattle's maritime world and striking views of the downtown skyline across Lake Union.

Distance: 2.8 miles out and back
Hiking time: About 1.5 hours
Difficulty: Easy, flat trail
Trail surface: Paved
Best season: Year-round
Other trail users: Bicyclists, skaters
Canine compatibility: Leashed dogs permitted

Fees and permits: No fees or permits required
Schedule: Open daily, 4 a.m. to 11:30 p.m.
Maps: USGS Seattle North E; Seattle street map
Trail contact: Seattle Parks and Recreation; (206) 684-4075; www.seattle.gov/parks
Special considerations: None

Finding the trailhead: From I-5 take exit 169 (Northeast 45th Street) and drive west on Northeast 45th Street. Turn left onto Burke Avenue North and travel until the road ends at North Northlake Way. You will see Gas Works Park across the street. Turn into the park parking lot (4-hour limit). Begin your hike across the street at the base of the Wallingford Steps. The beginning of the trail runs parallel to North Northlake Way. Facing the steps, follow the trail to the left. GPS: N47 38.82' / W122 20.19'

The Hike

Gas Works Park, on the north shore of Lake Union, is a Seattle destination in itself. If time allows before you hit the trail, explore the park with its kite hill and the relics of the old gasworks that adorn the picnic and children's play areas. It's a perfect example of how a cleaned-up industrial site can be reclaimed and put to good use. Here you'll enjoy views of this urban lake flanked by Capitol Hill on one side and Queen Anne Hill on the other, with the downtown skyline straight ahead.

Begin your hike on the paved trail across the street from the park. Facing away from the park, follow the trail to the left (west). Heavily used by bicyclists, the Burke-Gilman Trail is divided into two lanes—one for wheels and the other for feet—but sometimes the line between the lanes fades. Posted signs remind bicyclists that pedestrians have the right-of-way, but it's always a good idea to yield to bikes for your own safety.

The trail passes between a cement retaining wall and a chain-link fence, and here you might be hoping the entire trail isn't this ugly. Be patient. Soon the trail crosses Stone Way North at North 34th Street; continue on between the retaining wall and the Seattle Rowing Club and turn left. The scenery opens up.

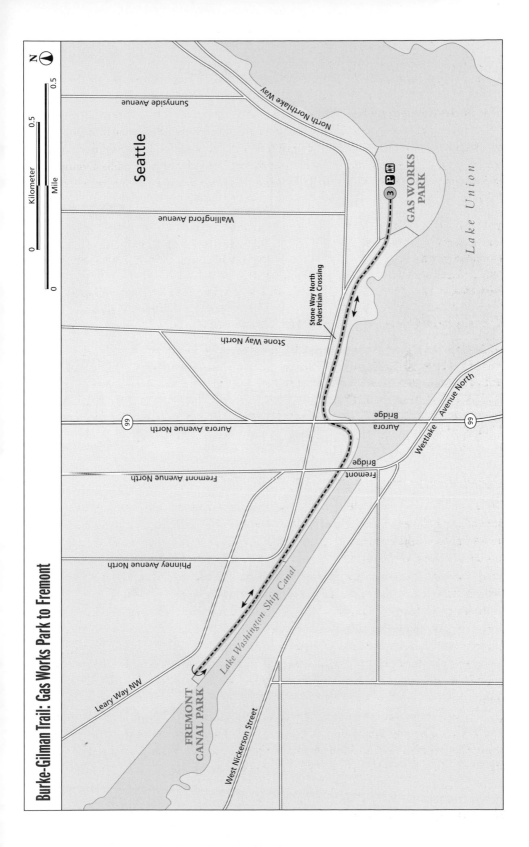

Burke-Gilman Trail: Gas Works Park to Fremont

Seattle

Lake Union

GAS WORKS PARK

Lake Washington Ship Canal

FREMONT CANAL PARK

Sunnyside Avenue

North Northlake Way

Wallingford Avenue

Stone Way North

Stone Way North Pedestrian Crossing

Aurora Avenue North

99

Aurora Bridge

Westlake Avenue North

99

Fremont Avenue North

Fremont Bridge

Phinney Avenue North

Leary Way NW

West Nickerson Street

N

0   0.5   Kilometer   0.5

0   Mile   0.5

Lake Union flows into the Fremont Cut of the Lake Washington Ship Canal. The shore is lined with houseboats (not really boats at all, but floating homes), tugs, sailboats, and fishing trawlers—if it floats, it's here. The imposing Aurora Bridge dominates the sky directly overhead.

The trail passes beneath the Aurora Bridge and then under the smaller, more colorful Fremont Bridge, built in 1916. Brand-name high-tech corporate campuses line the trail as it parallels the canal, continuing west. The trail passes a plaza with natural stone sculptures and another area with ivy dinosaurs and a kiosk with a supply of free *Fremont Walking Tour* brochures.

(**Option:** If you have time, this is a great place to detour 1 block away from the route and explore the eclectic and artsy Fremont District, which proudly proclaims itself the Center of the Universe.)

When you reach Fremont Canal Park, with its metal-grate deck and shelter suspended on the hillside between the trail and the canal, turn around and head back to your starting point at Gas Works Park.

Miles and Directions

0.0 Start at the base of the Wallingford Steps on North Northlake Way, across the street from Gas Works Park. There is no trailhead marker. Facing the paved trail with your back to Gas Works Park, begin your hike to the left (west).

0.4 Reach the intersection of Stone Way North and North 34th Street. Cross with the pedestrian traffic light and continue to follow the trail, which parallels North 34th Street behind a cement retaining wall.

0.6 The trail turns left, approaches Lake Union, and passes under the Aurora Bridge.

0.8 The trail passes under the Fremont Bridge and continues on, paralleling the Fremont Cut.

1.4 Reach the end of Fremont Canal Park (Northwest Canal Street and Second Avenue NW). Retrace your steps to the trailhead.

2.8 Arrive back at Gas Works Park.

◀ *Dogs are welcome in Gas Works Park.* © ISTOCK.COM/JULY7TH

4 Magnuson Park

Warren G. Magnuson Park occupies the site of the former Sand Point Naval Air Station on Lake Washington. When the base was closed, the city of Seattle acquired the land and buildings, making good use of the waterfront and wide-open spaces for public recreational and athletic facilities, including miles of trails.

Distance: 2.6-mile lollipop
Hiking time: About 1.5 hours
Difficulty: Easy, with one hill
Trail surface: Paved, gravel
Best season: Year-round
Other trail users: Bicyclists, skaters
Canine compatibility: Leashed dogs permitted; large off-leash area nearby
Fees and permits: No fees or permits required

Schedule: Open year-round; May 1 through Labor Day, 4 a.m. to 11:30 p.m.; Labor Day through Apr 30, 4 a.m. to 10 p.m.
Maps: USGS Seattle North E, Bellevue North W; Seattle street map
Trail contact: Seattle Parks and Recreation; (206) 684-4075; www.seattle.gov/parks
Special considerations: None

Finding the trailhead: From downtown Seattle drive north on I-5 and take exit 169 (Northeast 45th Street). Turn right onto Northeast 45th Street and follow it past the University of Washington and down the hill. The street becomes Sandpoint Way NE and curves to the left. Turn right at Northeast 65th Street, which ends at the Magnuson Park parking lot. The trailhead is to the left of the boat ramp as you face the lake. GPS: N47 40.55' / W122 15.04'

The Hike

Lake Washington stretches 20 miles along Seattle's entire eastern border and beyond, its shoreline home to miles of promenades, parks, bicycle trails, waterfront homes, neighborhood commercial districts, a hydroplane racing pit, the on-ramps of two floating bridges, and even the site of a former naval air station. When the Sand Point Naval Air Station closed, the city of Seattle seized the opportunity to acquire the lakefront property to create Magnuson Park, which now shares Sand Point with the National Oceanographic and Atmospheric Administration (NOAA).

Magnuson Park contains miles of trails. This hike follows the lakefront promenade, ascends Sand Point Head (aka Kite Hill), and circles a hilltop field with excellent views up and down the lake, east to the city of Kirkland, and beyond to the Cascade Mountains.

About midway along the promenade, you will notice something resembling killer whale dorsal fins—twenty-two of them in all—breaching the lawn as it gently rolls like waves. These are actually black diving fins from decommissioned US Navy attack submarines buried in the hillside, creating a provocative art installation titled *The Fin Project: From Swords into Plowshares.*

The promenade ends at a gate leading to a high point of the hike for your canine companion: an enormous fenced off-leash area that meanders through the park. This

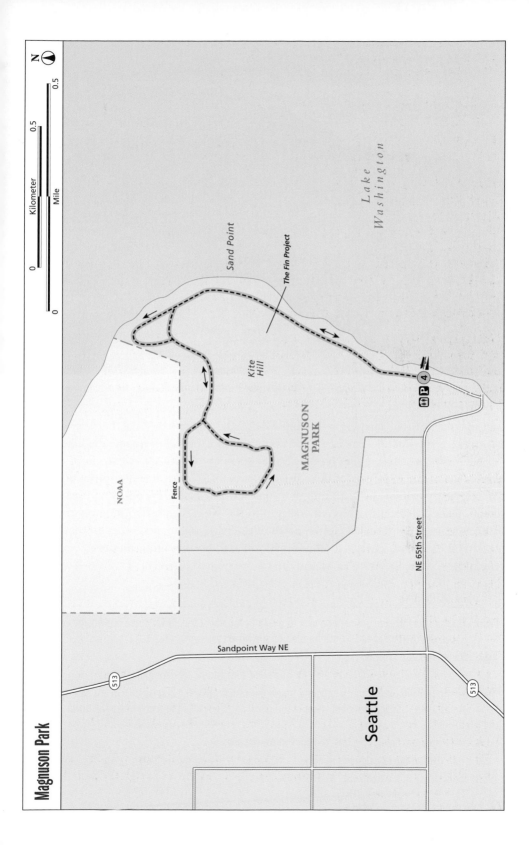

Magnuson Park

Sand Point

The Fin Project

Kite Hill

MAGNUSON PARK

NOAA

Fence

Lake Washington

Sandpoint Way NE

513

NE 65th Street

513

Seattle

Kilometer
0.5   0.5

Mile
0.5   0.5

0   0

N

Aerial view of Magnuson Park and Lake Washington, with Mount Rainier in the distance
© ISTOCK.COM/SEASTOCK

optional delight for your dog will temporarily take you off the trail, but you can backtrack, easily find the gate again, and continue up Kite Hill to resume the hike.

A nearby attraction resides on the secured grounds of NOAA: the lakefront Art Walk. One of the highlights of the collection is *Sound Garden*, a collection of pipes that play eerie sounds in the wind, the tone and pitch determined by the wind's direction and velocity. To access Art Walk, go to the NOAA security gate on Northeast 63rd Avenue, immediately to the north of the park, and request access to the Art Walk. If the current security level permits, you will go through a routine security screening, be issued a visitor's pass, and then be permitted to enter.

Miles and Directions

0.0 Start at the lakeside promenade next to the boat launch at the park's south parking lot. Cross the footbridge and follow the promenade north.

0.4 The trail passes The Fin Project, an art installation.

0.7 The trail reaches the off-leash area for dogs and turns to the left along the fence.

0.8 At the trail intersection, turn right and follow the trail up Kite Hill and beyond to the athletic fields. Circle the field for great views of the park, and then take the same trail back down the hill.

1.9 Walk straight through the trail intersection toward the lake.

2.0 Turn right at the lakeside promenade and walk south toward the trailhead.

2.6 Arrive back at the trailhead.

5 Lake Serene

Where the North and South Fork Skykomish Rivers come together, passengers in cars motoring along US 2 are treated to an amazing sight. To the south, all eyes find it hard to miss the Yosemite-like visual delight of Bridal Veil Falls leaping 1,000 feet into space in a series of foamy cataracts from its source in Lake Serene. Visiting the lake during the week or in the off-season, it's a serene experience as well, albeit a tough and exhausting one. But Lake Serene and Bridal Veil Falls are extremely popular places to visit, so hikers must be in a sharing mode on weekends. Once at the lake, be prepared for the jaw-dropping sight of Mount Index towering 3,500 feet above, dominating the scene.

Distance: 7.4 miles out and back

Hiking time: 4–5 hours

Difficulty: Difficult; most steep sections surmounted by stairs

Trail surface: Sometimes rocky forested path, boardwalk, stairs

Best season: Summer and fall

Other trail users: None

Canine compatibility: Dogs must be leashed when in or around developed recreation sites, trailheads, interpretive trails, or campgrounds; voice control allowed in forest and wilderness areas. Always check at the trailhead for specific information regarding leash vs. voice control regulations.

Fees and permits: Northwest Forest Pass required

Schedule: Open 24/7

Maps: Green Trails No.142: Index; USGS Index; USDAFS Mount Baker-Snoqualmie National Forest, Alpine Lakes Wilderness; *DeLorme: Washington Atlas and Gazetteer:* Page 80 B-4

Trail contacts: Alpine Lakes Protection Society (ALPS); www.alpinelakes.org. Mount Baker-Snoqualmie National Forest, Skykomish Ranger District, 74920 NE Stevens Pass Hwy., PO Box 305, Skykomish 98288; (360) 677-2414; www.fs.fed.us/r6/mbs/about/srd.shtml.

Special considerations: Loose rock, exposure (stay within guardrails near Bridal Veil Falls); no potable water at trailhead or on trail

Finding the trailhead: From Seattle take WA 522 to Monroe, turning (left) east onto US 2. Drive US 2 through Gold Bar, passing signs to Wallace Falls State Park at First Avenue. Continue east for another 7.3 miles to Mount Index Road (FR 6020). Turn right (south) onto a wide, potholed unpaved road. Drive 0.2 mile and bear right (south) at a fork onto FR 6020-109. Continue 0.1 mile to a parking area. GPS: N47 48.55' / W121 34.42'

The Hike

The current trail to Lake Serene is not the trail that many old-time hikers in the region remember. That thing—hardly a trail at all—was an outrageously extraordinary up-and-down excursion into the fifth dimension across Utah-style slickrock and moon-size tree roots. Enough people were hauled down that old trail, blubbering on the verge of a nervous breakdown, that generations of guidebooks kept Lake Serene out of their pages.

A highway-viewable waterfall flowing from Lake Serene PETER STEKEL

No more. A new trail has changed it all. Not that some of the old trail features have disappeared completely!

The steep trail to Lake Serene seems unending—especially during the long, hot summer days that periodically sit over the Puget Sound region. Maybe that's why

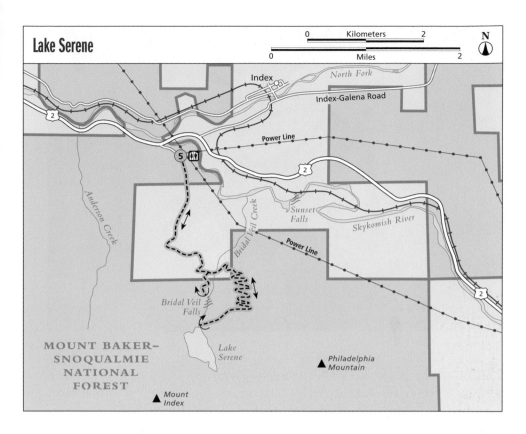

the trail, which feels as though it reaches from the depths of some bottomless hole and into the heavens, is so unbearable to so many people who come equipped for a backyard barbecue versus a strenuous hike.

From the parking area, walk around the gate on what is obviously an old road. After 0.1 mile bear right (south) at the hiker sign. Many of the old volunteer trails still exist—though the yearly renewable flagging is long, long gone. Keep your eyes sharp, and follow the main route to avoid getting off course.

Cross a small creek; in another 0.3 mile cross it again. Believe it or not, cars used to come this far. After 1.2 miles from the trailhead, another sign directs hikers to the right (south) on a wide, obvious trail. Another fork and another trail sign in 0.1 mile direct hikers left (southeast). In another 0.1 mile the trail bears left (southeast) at another fork. Turning the opposite direction leads to Bridal Veil Falls. It's worth the detour. On a hot day the spray of water is most refreshing. Stay within the guardrails, since the slope is wet and slippery. One false step could be embarrassing, to say the least. Tired hikers stop at the falls, turn around, and head home.

Returning to the main trail, a series of stairs continues the trail down to a stream, crossing on a sturdy bridge with an even sturdier handrail. After that the trail climbs. And climbs. Switchbacks take the trail west until it reaches a lip below the lake. All of

© ISTOCK.COM/TNTEMERSON

a sudden there it is: Lake Serene. It's difficult to know where to look first. The lake is certainly inviting—especially for hikers flushed in the face from the steep and direct climb. But Mount Index so dramatically overlords the view that it isn't easy to keep your eyes from drifting toward the sky.

After reaching the lake, boardwalks head out in both directions. People (and dogs) like to swim in the lake on hot days, and it isn't hard to understand why—though the water is very cold. It's all snowmelt, you know.

To return, retrace your steps down the trail—and marvel at how almost vertical it was on the way up. Hopefully a walking stick will slow down the declivitous descent. Only dogs capable of navigating steep, rocky trail sections should be brought along on this hike.

Miles and Directions

0.0   Start at the trailhead on FR 6020-109.

0.1   Bear right (south) at the hiker sign.

1.2   Bear right (south) on a wide, obvious trail.

1.3   Bear left (southeast) at a fork.

1.4   Come to another fork; bear right for the detour to Bridal Veil Falls.

1.8   Reach Bridal Veil Falls. Return to the main trail.

3.7   Arrive at Lake Serene. Retrace your steps to the trailhead.

7.4   Arrive back at the trailhead.

6 Preston-Snoqualmie Trail: Lake Alice to Snoqualmie Falls Overlook

Nearly 100 feet higher than Niagara Falls, Snoqualmie Falls drops from a height of 268 feet; the width varies based on the time of year and the amount of rainfall. The site of the falls attracts 1.5 million visitors a year, but from the Preston–Snoqualmie Trail, you're likely to have the view of the falls all to yourself.

Distance: 3.6 miles out and back
Hiking time: 1.5–2 hours
Difficulty: Easy, flat trail with one gentle incline
Trail surface: Paved
Best season: Year-round; winter rains adds volume to the falls.
Other trail users: Bicyclists, skaters
Canine compatibility: Leashed dogs permitted

Fees and permits: No fees or permits required
Schedule: Open year-round, dawn to dusk
Maps: USGS Fall City, Snoqualmie; King County street map
Trail contact: King County Parks and Recreation; (206) 296-8687; www.kingcounty.gov/services/parks-recreation/parks.aspx
Special considerations: None

Finding the trailhead: From Seattle drive east on I-90 and take exit 22. Turn left and drive over the overpass. Turn right at the first intersection and drive through Preston. The road becomes Preston–Fall City Road SE. Turn right onto Southeast 47th Street and then right onto Lake Alice Road. Drive up the hill until you reach the well-signed trailhead; turn right into the parking lot. GPS: N47 33.05' / W121 53.23'

The Hike

Snoqualmie Falls is the site of the region's first hydroelectric plant, built in 1898. Still in operation, the plant provides the Seattle metropolitan area with much of its power.

This paved, straight, gradually graded trail begins in a residential area in rural King County, but soon the residential properties thin out and the trail follows the side of wooded Snoqualmie Ridge high above the Raging and Snoqualmie River valleys. In spite of the trail's proximity to civilization, a sign at the trailhead with graphics of a bear and cougar remind you that you are treading into wildlife habitat.

The trail follows a historic railroad grade (as do many of the region's trails) that played a major role in populating the fertile valleys at the foot of the Cascades as well as transporting timber and coal. Today there's no visible evidence of the area's timber and railroad history along this portion of the Preston-Snoqualmie Trail.

History buffs will enjoy a separate visit to the trail's nearby namesake towns: the historic sawmill town of Preston and the railroad town of Snoqualmie, home to the Northwest Railroad Museum, with its period depot and impressive collection of vintage railroad cars lining the main street.

If treading in a place that had a hand in shaping the region's history doesn't entice you, the view at the end of the trail surely will: the long drop of Snoqualmie Falls, the

Preston-Snoqualmie Trail: Lake Alice to Snoqualmie Falls Overlook

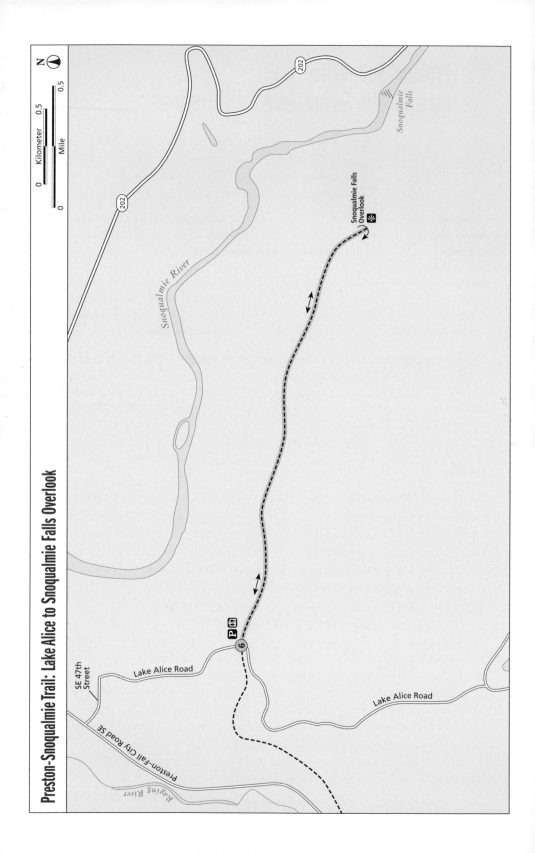

Snoqualmie Falls as seen from downriver © ISTOCK.COM/GMC3101

visitor center and lodge perched at the top of the falls, and the jagged Cascade peaks rising above it all.

Miles and Directions

0.0 Start at the trailhead, which is across Lake Alice Road from the parking lot.

0.5 Gradually descend into a shallow ravine and out again.

0.7 Pass a viewpoint with benches overlooking the Snoqualmie Valley.

1.8 The trail dead-ends at the Snoqualmie Falls overlook. Retrace your steps to the trailhead.

3.6 Arrive back at the trailhead.

7 Snow Lake

The popular (25,000 annual visitors) route up to Snow Lake swarms with people during summer, and finding a place to hang out along the lake's rocky beach is close to impossible on sunny weekends. Still, the lake sits within a gorgeous setting and should not be missed. A fall excursion to pick huckleberries is bound to find fewer people on the trail. Such is the popularity of the lake that even a rainy day sees plenty of visitors but at least no crowds. In spring, fields of wildflowers bloom at regular intervals along the trail—another reason for the lake's popularity.

Distance: 7.0 miles out and back
Hiking time: About 6 hours
Difficulty: Moderate, with steep areas
Trail surface: Forested path; rocky
Best season: Summer and fall
Other trail users: Llamas and goats
Canine compatibility: Dogs must be leashed when in or around developed recreation sites, trailheads, interpretive trails, or campgrounds; voice control allowed in forest and wilderness areas. Always check at the trailhead for specific information regarding leash vs. voice control regulations.
Fees and permits: Northwest Forest Pass required

Schedule: Open 24/7
Maps: Green Trails No. 207: Snoqualmie Pass; USGS Snoqualmie Pass; USDAFS Mount Baker–Snoqualmie National Forest, Alpine Lakes Wilderness; *DeLorme: Washington Atlas and Gazetteer:* Page 65 A-5
Trail contacts: Alpine Lakes Protection Society (ALPS): www.alpinelakes.org. Middle Fork Snoqualmie; www.midforc.org. Mount Baker–Snoqualmie National Forest, Snoqualmie Ranger District, North Bend Office, 42404 SE North Bend Way, North Bend 98045; (425) 888-1421; www.fs.fed.us/r6/mbs/recreation.
Special considerations: Loose rock; no potable water at trailhead or on trail

Finding the trailhead: From Seattle drive east on I-90 and take exit 52 (west summit to Snoqualmie Pass). Turn left (north) onto FR 9040 (unmarked) and then turn right (north) at Alpental Road, the second street. After 1.5 miles enter a large gravel parking lot used by Alpental ski area. Park in the northernmost section of the lot. There is a vault toilet hidden behind some trees. GPS: N47 26.70' / W121 25.42'

The Hike

Cross Alpental Road from the parking area (no public access is allowed past the car park) and find the marked trailhead. There is a self-registration station for Alpine Lakes Wilderness and an information kiosk. Climb a series of stairs constructed of logs, which finally ends at a rocky trail that traverses the hillside across several avalanche chutes. The area around Snoqualmie Pass is part of the Naches Formation, volcanic rocks interlaid with sandstone that were deposited around forty-five million years ago. There are good exposures of Eocene andesite in the cliffs and rocks around these chutes.

The trees around here are big. If hiking the Puget Sound lowlands has taken the edge off experiencing western hemlock enjoy these big boys—they are mountain

Snow Lake PETER STEKEL

hemlock. The cones are much smaller than their lowland relatives, and the tree needles lack the distinctive starburst appearance of western hemlock. Both species share the characteristic tree crown, which bends over like a limp wrist.

Ascend through the forest and avalanche chutes, cross talus fields, and in 2.0 miles reach the Source Lake Overlook Trail junction. This 1.0-mile round-trip spur trail takes hikers across rock slopes to look down upon the source of South Fork Snoqualmie River.

Continuing east and north to Snow Lake, the trail begins to switchback uphill. The sometimes-rocky trail rises upslope, at times crossing the same avalanche chute visited below. The upper part of the trail is replaced in steeper areas by log steps. Cross the Alpine Lakes Wilderness boundary at 2.5 miles; cross over the lip into Snow Lake basin and begin to descend.

The lake is visible through the trees as the trail crosses a talus field and keeps on dropping. Above the lakeshore is a sign, perhaps left by Paul Bunyan, directing hikers

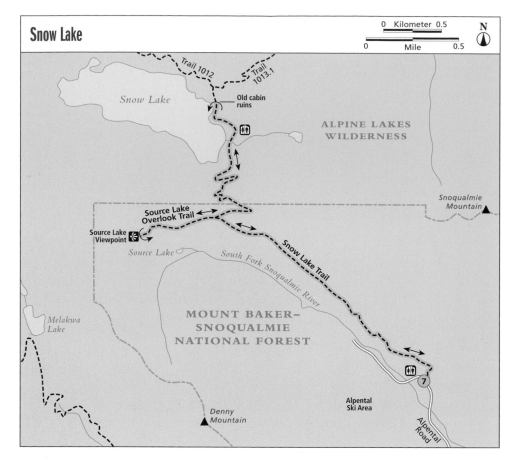

0   Kilometer 0.5

0   Mile   0.5

N

Trail 1012

Trail 1013.1

Snow Lake

Old cabin ruins

ALPINE LAKES WILDERNESS

Source Lake Overlook Trail

Snoqualmie Mountain

Source Lake Viewpoint

Source Lake

South Fork Snoqualmie River

Snow Lake Trail

Melakwa Lake

MOUNT BAKER– SNOQUALMIE NATIONAL FOREST

7

Alpental Ski Area

Denny Mountain

Alpental Road

to campsites, the main trail, and ruins of a stone-walled cabin and cautioning everyone that no fires are allowed.

Walk past the toilet, a cute waterfall and pool, lots of blocked-off waytrails, and the vaguely delimited main trail that continues on up the valley. Reach the cabin ruins—a house really, and a large one at that. Many of the rock walls are still standing, as is what must have been a very nice fireplace. Campsites and lake access lie below.

It's impossible to hike in the Pacific Northwest without spending some time walking in the rain. There are advantages to this! In popular places like Snow Lake, expect fewer people on the trails. Rain walking is a great opportunity to leave your stuffy house, and it beats being cooped up all day. In autumn there are huckleberries to pick and fall colors to enjoy. And at the end of the day, no matter how wet you are, you can always go home and take a hot shower. Just make sure you come prepared for wet weather by bringing along the best rain gear you can afford, plenty of warm (and dry) clothes, food, and energy snacks.

Campsites at Snow Lake are poor, and many of the best are now prohibited from use so that the ground can recover from generations of heavy abuse. No fires are

© ISTOCK.COM/SOLOVYOVA

allowed, and group size is limited to twelve. Good luck, though, finding ample camping close to one another if you have a group that big.

On the return, retrace your steps down the Snow Lake Trail. At the junction with the trail to Source Lake Overlook, detour 0.5 mile to admire the cliffs and numerous creeks where South Fork Snoqualmie River begins. Come back to the main trail, and keep heading downhill to the parking lot at Alpental.

Miles and Directions

0.0 Start at the trailhead at the Alpental parking lot.

2.0 Pass the Source Lake Overlook Trail junction.

2.5 Reach the Alpine Lakes Wilderness boundary.

3.0 Come to an old cabin (ruins).

3.0 Arrive at Snow Lake. Retrace your steps to the Source Lake Overlook junction and detour to the viewpoint.

4.5 Reach the Source Lake Overlook. Return to the main trail and head back to the trailhead.

7.0 Arrive back at the trailhead.

8 Lake Lillian

Because it begins by climbing a clear-cut hillside, this isn't as popular a route as found elsewhere around Snoqualmie Pass. But that prejudice aside, the trail soon enters an old-growth forest and leads to a beautiful lake surrounded by awesome cliffs and craggy mountains. Along the way are dynamite views across the spine of the Cascades plus a shot at Mount Rainier. Wildflowers are abundant during summer in wet meadows surrounding Twin Lakes and the talus field below Lake Lillian.

Distance: 9.0 miles out and back
Hiking time: 6–7 hours
Difficulty: Difficult, with sections of narrow trail that are straight up and down
Trail surface: Forested path; rocky
Best season: Summer and fall
Other trail users: Illegal use by mountain bikers is a problem on this hikers-only trail.
Canine compatibility: Dogs must be leashed when in or around developed recreation sites, trailheads, interpretive trails, or campgrounds; voice control allowed in forest and wilderness areas. Always check at the trailhead for specific information regarding leash vs. voice control regulations.
Fees and permits: Northwest Forest Pass required
Schedule: Open 24/7

Maps: Green Trails No. 207: Snoqualmie Pass; USGS Chikamin Peak; USDAFS Mount Baker-Snoqualmie National Forest, Alpine Lakes Wilderness; *DeLorme: Washington Atlas and Gazetteer:* Page 65 A-6
Trail contacts: Alpine Lakes Protection Society (ALPS): www.alpinelakes.org. Middle Fork Snoqualmie: www.midforc.org. Wenatchee National Forest, Cle Elum Ranger District, 803 W. Second St., Cle Elum 98922; (509) 852-1100; www.fs.fed.us/r6/wenatchee. Mount Baker-Snoqualmie National Forest, Snoqualmie Ranger District, North Bend Office, 42404 SE North Bend Way, North Bend 98045; (425) 888-1421; www.fs.fed.us/r6/mbs/recreation.
Special considerations: Loose rock; no potable water at trailhead or on trail

Finding the trailhead: From Seattle take I-90 east to exit 54 (Gold Creek). Turn left (north) at the end of the off-ramp. Proceed 0.2 mile, go under the interstate, and pass the on-ramp to I-90 westbound. Turn right (east) on Gold Creek Road (FR 4832) and begin paralleling I-90. After 2 miles the road narrows to one lane, becoming gravel at 2.4 miles. At 2.7 miles the road makes a switchback, leaving I-90 behind.

Though the road is in good shape, consider bringing some laundry—it's heavily washboarded. The road climbs steadily to another switchback at 3.7 miles and then another switchback at 3.9 miles and a fork in the road. Bear left onto FR 4934, following the road sign to Trail 1332. The road narrows, switchbacks at 4.3 miles, and switchbacks again at 4.4 miles. Continue straight ahead (northwest) into the Mount Margaret parking area. The sounds of I-90 can be heard faintly below. GPS: N47 21.799' / W121 21.369'

The Hike

To find the trailhead, leave the parking lot and turn left (north), returning to FR 4934. Walk 0.2 mile up the road and take the gated spur road to the left (east). Begin

Small meadow along the trail to Lake Lillian PETER STEKEL

walking along this old road through a forest of vine maple, willow, red alder, and maturing Douglas fir and mountain hemlock. Stay on the main road despite opportunities to turn off until reaching a junction marked by a fiberglass forest service stick-sign announcing a hikers–only trail. An older metal sign bolted onto a 4 × 4-inch, 8-foot-tall post declares that this trail is closed to motor vehicles, saddle horses, and pack stock. Turn north, then east onto a narrow trail and climb through a regenerating clear-cut. As the trail climbs there are plenty of vistas east, west, and south to such familiar sights as I-90, Mount Rainier, Keechelus Lake, and the ski slopes of Snoqualmie Pass.

Keechelus Lake is also known by the sobriquet "Stump Lake" for its prevalence of tree stumps exposed in wintertime when the reservoir is low. A 128-foot-tall earth-fill structure, built in 1917 and operated by the US Bureau of Reclamation, controls the lake capacity and discharge for agriculture. Keechelus, which is supposed to mean "few fish" in the local Indian dialect, is the source of the Yakima River. Downstream is Kachess Lake, which supposedly means "more fish."

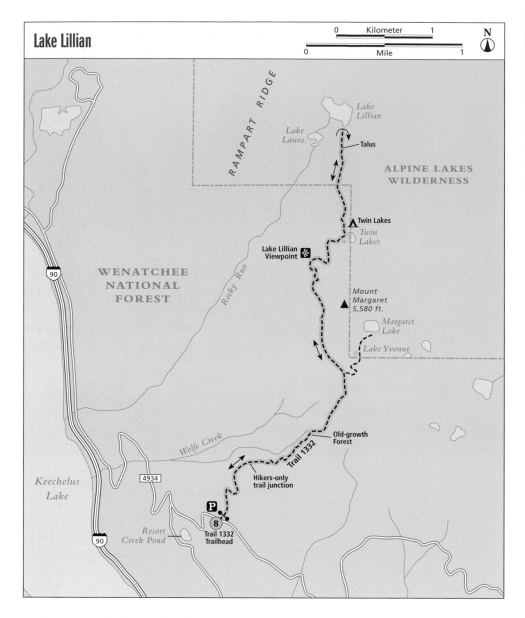

0   Kilometer   1

0   Mile   1

N

Lake
Lillian

Lake
Laura

Talus

RAMPART RIDGE

ALPINE LAKES
WILDERNESS

90

WENATCHEE
NATIONAL
FOREST

Rocky Run

Twin Lakes

Twin
Lakes

Lake Lillian
Viewpoint

Mount
Margaret
5,580 ft.

Margaret
Lake

Lake Yvonne

Old-growth
Forest

Wolfe Creek

Trail 1332

Hikers-only
trail junction

4934

Keechelus
Lake

P

8

Resort
Creek Pond

Trail 1332
Trailhead

90

Cross an old dirt road and continue up the trail. After nearly 2.0 miles from the parking area, enter an old-growth forest and begin a series of nicely graded switchbacks. In 2.5 miles reach the top of a ridge and the junction to Margaret Lake on the right (east). Continue straight ahead (north). Pass several waytrails (northeast) that lead to views of Rampart Ridge.

The trail skirts below the summits of two peaks, including Mount Margaret, and reaches a viewpoint. More of Rampart Ridge can be seen, along with a piece of Lake Lillian, a couple of ribbon waterfalls, and Rocky Run, the stream that drains the lake.

Begin descending toward Twin Lakes on a trail that sometimes could use a ladder. In 1.0 mile reach the lakes and cross into the Alpine Lakes Wilderness.

Twin Lakes are small and shallow and seasonally provide beautiful habitat for large hordes of mosquitoes. The first lake is the larger of the two and has a poor campsite about midway up the lake—though the scenery is nice. Some people choose to camp on a small island close to shore. This is a bad idea and is discouraged, since it's impossible to get 100 feet away from water in any direction—a requirement for good campers everywhere.

Leaving the larger lake, the trail follows a creek to the smaller lake and traverses even better mosquito habitat. Climb steeply and in earnest for a short while, and then proceed to lose elevation as the trail avoids having to deal with some heinous cliffs. Cross through a wide talus field and regain all the elevation lost since passing the Margaret Lake Trail junction. A brief flat spot is reached before you ascend the remaining part of the hillside—straight up! Where's that ladder?

It's not a long climb, fortunately, before the trail reaches a lip; in 100 feet Lake Lillian pops into view, surrounded by an amphitheater of rock and jagged peaks. There is no place to go from here except for mountain goats and rock climbers.

Camping sites, located back at the lip, are paltry and far from level. Impressive views down the cliffs to Lake Laura, Rocky Run, clear-cuts, and FR 136 are nearby. Return to the trailhead by the same route.

Miles and Directions

0.0   Start at the trailhead off FR 4934.

0.5   Junction with hikers-only trail.

1.0   Cross dirt road.

2.0   Enter old-growth forest.

2.5   At the Lake Lillian/Margaret Lake Trail junction, stay straight.

3.5   Reach the Alpine Lakes Wilderness boundary and Twin Lakes.

4.0   Cross a talus field.

4.5   Reach Lake Lillian; retrace your steps to the trailhead.

9.0   Arrive back at the trailhead.

9 Mirror Lake

Tall trees, a sharp peak, and a flowery waterfall surround this gem of a lake just over 1 mile from the trailhead. Mirror Lake is a popular destination for the first-time backpacker because it's a short hike with a destination as beautiful as dozens of more popular lakes in the Alpine Lakes Wilderness north of Snoqualmie Pass.

Distance: 3.0 miles out and back
Hiking time: About 1.5 hours
Difficulty: Easy
Trail surface: Dirt trail
Best season: July–Oct
Other trail users: None
Canine compatibility: Dogs must be leashed when in or around developed recreation sites, trailheads, interpretive trails, or campgrounds; voice control allowed in forest and wilderness areas. Always check at the trailhead for specific information regarding leash vs. voice control regulations.
Fees and permits: Northwest Forest Pass required to park at trailhead
Schedule: Open 24/7
Map: Green Trails No. 207: Snoqualmie Pass
Trail contact: Okanogon-Wenatchee National Forest, Cle Elum Ranger District; (509) 852-1100; www.fs.usda.gov/okawen
Special considerations: None

Finding the trailhead: From Snoqualmie Pass drive east for 10 miles on I-90 to exit 62. Turn right at the bottom of the off-ramp and drive over the Yakima River; pass Stampede Gravel and turn right onto FR 5480, 1.1 miles from the exit. Reach an intersection at 5.2 miles from I-90 and take a soft right to continue on FR 5480. This intersection is confusing, but you'll soon see Lost Lake; if you are on the right (north) side of the lake, you'll know you're on the correct road. From here the road begins climbing along the right (north) side of Lost Lake. At 7.1 miles from I-90, park on the wide shoulder on the left side of the road, or continue up a rougher section of road for 0.3 mile to the upper parking lot. GPS: N47 20.760' / W121 25.467'

The Hike

A herculean trek through virgin wilderness this is not. But it is a peaceful nook where you can enjoy the woods without a strenuous hike. If a short hike to an alpine lake is what you're looking for, look no farther than Mirror Lake. Even though it's close to the trailhead, Mirror Lake is every bit as beautiful as many other lakes in the nearby Alpine Lakes Wilderness.

The hike to this peaceful lake is a gentle stroll through a moss-draped forest of big trees, sparse understory, and pools of clear water. Several campsites along both Mirror and Cottonwood Lakes make this a great first backpacking trip that is doable with kids, dogs, and lots of gear. Just beyond the lake, the trail leaves the old-growth forest and enters a clear-cut that extends toward a patchwork of trees and more clear-cuts on the horizon. A trail winds down through a young forest alongside a waterfall at the lake outlet. The stream cascades down toward Twilight Lake. The young trees on this open hillside allow plenty of sunlight to reach a garden of crimson columbines,

Mirror Lake beneath Tinkham Peak OLIVER LAZENBY

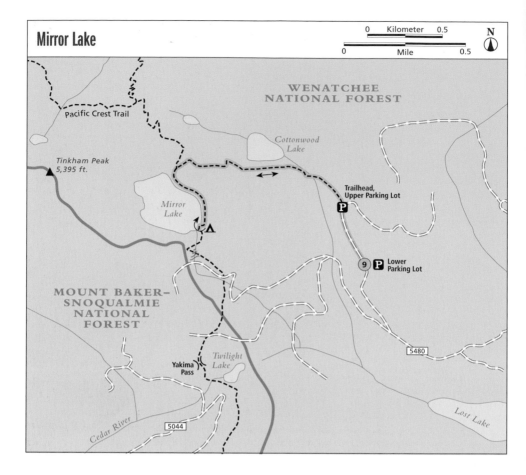

Columbia lilies, Indian paintbrush, bear grass, asters, and lupines. The scene here looks like an impressionist painting—the view down to Yakima Pass is a smudgy palette of green with dots of red, orange, yellow, and purple in the foreground.

While tranquil, high-alpine lakes are plentiful near Snoqualmie Pass, nice hikes are rare in this heavily logged area south of I-90. Much of the north side of I-90 at Snoqualmie Pass is blessed with wilderness status, as the Alpine Lakes Wilderness stretches nearly to the interstate in some areas. The south side of I-90 does not enjoy this protection. It is USDA Forest Service land and is heavily logged. On the path to Mirror Lake, however, you'll walk through a forest of big firs spared the cables and saws. Amid these trees you can gaze into the glassy water of the lake and contemplate the reflection of Tinkham Peak and its jagged flanks—a popular scramble for those with experience and no fear of heights.

From the unsigned trailhead, take off through a couple open patches of vegetation and enjoy the smatterings of wildflowers. The trail climbs gently for most of its length. The trailside sights remain interesting, and in a little over 0.75 mile you reach

© ISTOCK.COM/BGSMITH

Cottonwood Lake, a glassy pool cradled by tall ridges. Less than 0.5 mile later, you reach a junction with the Pacific Crest Trail (PCT) right before reaching Mirror Lake. Turn left at the junction and continue toward the east bank of the lake.

Both Mirror Lake and Twilight Lake, which is 1.0 mile farther south on the PCT, are popular for fishing. Cottonwood Lake, on the way to Mirror Lake, is too shallow to support many fish.

Miles and Directions

0.0 Start from the lower parking spots on FR 5480.

0.3 Pass the upper parking lot and continue on the trail on the left (west) side of the road.

0.8 Reach Cottonwood Lake and continue to the left (south) of it.

1.2 Turn left (south) onto the Pacific Crest Trail toward Stampede Pass.

1.3 Arrive at Mirror Lake.

1.5 Reach the first campsite at the lake. Return the way you came.

3.0 Arrive back at the lower parking lot.

10 Taylor River

A walk along Taylor River is perfect for you and your pup during the two- or three-week period in summer when Seattle is suffocating in our yearly 80°F temperatures. Tree tunnels provide ample shade, and periodic use trails down to the river make for splashing opportunities. Water at Marten and Big Creeks is also available to wash off the sweat of the hike, and your dog will enjoy plenty of water to drink. The canyon is cool here from downcanyon drift.

The Taylor is a tributary of the Middle Fork Snoqualmie, and this trail (a long-abandoned road) follows above the river for 5 miles to the bridge over Big Creek. Along the way are side trails to Marten Lake and Otter Falls. Spring brings water to many side streams that cross the trail and feed two impressive waterfalls.

Distance: 10.0 miles out and back

Hiking time: About 5 hours

Difficulty: Moderate due to length

Trail surface: Forested path, gravel road; rocky; wide and gentle trail

Best season: Spring through fall

Other trail users: Bicyclists, equestrians, runners

Canine compatibility: Dogs must be leashed when in or around developed recreation sites, trailheads, interpretive trails, or campgrounds; voice control allowed in forest and wilderness areas. Always check at the trailhead for specific information regarding leash vs. voice control regulations.

Fees and permits: Northwest Forest Pass required

Schedule: Open 24/7

Maps: USGS Lake Philippa, Snoqualmie Lake; Green Trails No. 174: Mount Si and No. 175: Skykomish; USDAFS Mount Baker–Snoqualmie National Forest; *DeLorme: Washington Atlas and Gazetteer:* Page 64 A-2, 3.

Trail contacts: Alpine Lakes Protection Society (ALPS): www.alpinelakes.org. Middle Fork Snoqualmie: www.midforc.org. Mount Baker–Snoqualmie National Forest, Snoqualmie Ranger District, North Bend Office, 42404 SE North Bend Way, North Bend 98045; (425) 888-1421; www.fs.fed.us/r6/mbs/recreation.

Special considerations: Loose rock; no potable water at trailhead or on trail

Finding the trailhead: Drive east from Seattle to North Bend on I-90 to exit 34 (468th Avenue SE/Edgewick Road). During winter closures of Snoqualmie Pass, this is as far east as you can drive. Turn left (north) at the stop sign and proceed past a truck stop, gas stations, and a restaurant. In less than 1 mile arrive at Southeast Middle Fork Road (FR 56) and turn right (east). In 1 mile bear right at a Y junction onto Lake Dorothy Road. Pavement ends in 1.6 miles at a pullout and small parking lot for the Mailbox Peak Trail, and the road becomes FR 56 (FR 5600 on some maps).

After 2.6 miles on this good hardpack road with patches of gravel and occasional heavy zones of potholes, pass the popular Granite Creek put-in for kayakers. Cross a well-built concrete bridge and, in 2.1 miles, pass the Bessemer Mountain Trailhead. Pass the Middle Fork Snoqualmie River Trailhead in another 4.5 miles. Pass a forest service campground on your left (northeast), cross the Taylor River on a smaller concrete bridge, and turn left at a junction to reach the Snoqualmie Lake Trailhead in 1 mile.

The road ends here at a gate and a small parking area. If the lot is full, drive back 0.2 mile to the bridge and park in one of the wide spots along the road. GPS: N47 33.66' / W121 31.93'

Strolling by the river

The Hike

The 1921 USGS Sultan quad shows a ranger station just downstream of the confluence with the Taylor and Snoqualmie Rivers and a trail poking up the Middle Fork. Leave your car at the Snoqualmie Lake Trailhead and pass around the stout metal gate. Immediately on the right is a short trail down to a side channel of the Taylor. It has plenty of sitting spots for lunch and bountiful views up- and downstream. Some have even used it as an informal camping area. The tall trunks of a mature streamside red alder forest provide shade on hot days. To continue, return to Quartz Creek Road (the wide pathway).

A newly constructed heavy-duty wooden bridge crosses Marten Creek in 3.0 miles. Look left (north) for a small cairn beside the trail marking a use trail up to Marten Lake. The Taylor River Trail begins to narrow now from its earlier, wider character and crosses several streams. The trail is rough in parts but is never difficult to follow.

After 4.5 miles of hiking, another use trail left (north) beside the trail leads to Otter Falls and a nice swimming hole. In another 0.5 mile arrive at the Big Creek Bridge—incongruously large and overbuilt given the setting. Expect to see an amazing waterfall skittering down long slabs of rock throughout the year.

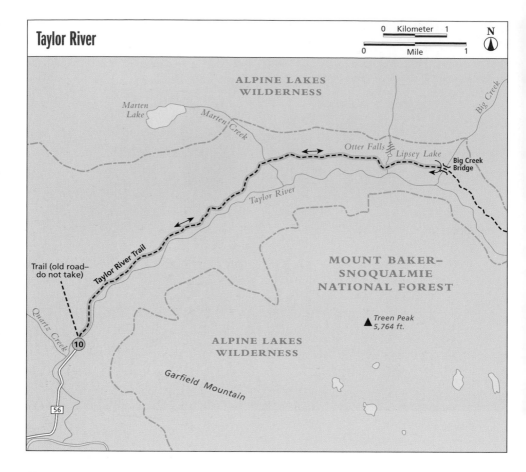

0   Kilometer   1

0   Mile   1

N

ALPINE LAKES
WILDERNESS

*Marten
Lake*

Marten Creek

Big Creek

Otter Falls

Lipsey Lake

**Big Creek
Bridge**

Taylor River

Trail (old road–
do not take)

Taylor River Trail

**MOUNT BAKER–
SNOQUALMIE
NATIONAL FOREST**

▲ *Treen Peak
5,764 ft.*

Quartz Creek

10

ALPINE LAKES
WILDERNESS

Garfield Mountain

56

Turn around and return to your car. It's possible to continue on to Dorothy Lake with a car shuttle at US 2 to lengthen your trip.

Miles and Directions

0.0   Start at the Snoqualmie Lake Trailhead (Taylor River Trail).

1.0   Quartz Creek Road.

3.0   Cross Marten Creek on a wooden bridge.

4.5   Pass the Otter Falls Trail junction.

5.0   Reach the Big Creek Bridge. Return the way you came.

10.0   Arrive back at the trailhead.

11 Kendall Katwalk

A cliff-side catwalk adds drama and views to this convenient-to-Seattle stretch of the Pacific Crest Trail. Bonus: There's plenty of water and shade to keep pups cool and hydrated on hot days.

Distance: 12.0 miles out and back
Hiking time: About 6 hours
Difficulty: Difficult due to length
Trail surface: Wide dirt path with a rocky traverse through talus
Best season: Mid-July–Oct
Other trail users: Equestrians, pack animals
Canine compatibility: Dogs must be leashed when in or around developed recreation sites, trailheads, interpretive trails, or campgrounds; voice control allowed in forest and wilderness areas. Always check at the trailhead for specific information regarding leash vs. voice control regulations.
Fees and permits: Northwest Forest Pass required to park at trailhead
Schedule: Open 24/7
Maps: USGS Snoqualmie Pass; Green Trails No. 206: Bandera
Trail contact: Mount Baker-Snoqualmie National Forest, North Bend Ranger District; (425) 888-1421
Special considerations: None

Finding the trailhead: From Seattle drive 52 miles east on I-90 to exit 52. Turn left at the bottom of the off-ramp and go under the freeway. In 0.1 mile take the first right onto a dirt road, following signs for the Pacific Crest Trail. The road splits into two parking areas. The lot to the right is closer to the trailhead, but either one works. GPS: N47 25.67' / W121 24.82'

The Hike

This entire hike is on the Pacific Crest Trail (PCT), and it's about as rugged and remote-feeling an area as you can find on a day trip near I-90. The trail starts at the top of Snoqualmie Pass and goes north for 6.0 beautiful miles, leaving the freeway far behind and probing into the Alpine Lakes Wilderness Area. The Katwalk itself is a unique feature—a narrow man-made shelf blasted into a 70-degree granite cliff. The view from the Katwalk is among the best near Snoqualmie Pass. From the Katwalk and the craggy upper sections of Kendall Peak—which the trail traverses—the freeway is out of sight and earshot, allowing hikers to experience the wilderness to the north in its silent, car-less glory. Combine that with views of distant peaks like Mount Stuart, which rears its head to the left of Alta Mountain, and this area feels expansive and wild. Along the way, dense patches of flowers between talus slopes burst to life after the snow finally melts.

The Kendall Katwalk was blasted into the granite knife edge in the late 1970s as part of rerouting a section of the PCT. The PCT, which stretches from Mexico to Canada, started as a series of regional trails. Washington's section was called the Cascade Crest Trail. Apparently the engineers of the PCT weren't impressed by the Cascade Crest Trail, which went over Red Pass and down to the Middle Fork

A hiker crossing the Kendall Katwalk OLIVER LAZENBY

Snoqualmie River valley, bypassing the high country north of the Katwalk. The trail was rerouted in the 1970s to bring it up to PCT standards. It now traverses a series of airy, steep slopes with spectacular views and incredible heights. Since the trail builders couldn't find a route around it, they blasted a trail through the slab with dynamite—and the Katwalk was born.

Most folks do the Katwalk as a day hike. The trek to the Katwalk and back makes for a long day, but the trail climbs gently the whole way and gains less elevation than the trails to many nearby peaks. Ridge, Gravel, and Alaska Lakes are just beyond the Katwalk for an even longer day or overnight destination.

From the parking lot, follow the PCT as it switchbacks and contours through a forest of hemlocks and firs. The wide and well-maintained path crosses back and forth over several streams. If it's very hot, be sure to fill water containers in these streams so you have your dog's water needs covered for the stream-free 6.0 miles out and back to the ridge. The trail climbs steadily through this section but never gets steep. The tall evergreen trees conceal the surrounding peaks for the first 2.0 miles until Guye Peak, an imposing rocky spire with 2,000-foot-tall rock faces, appears to your left.

From here you leave the biggest of the trees behind, cross several talus meadows, and lose a few hundred feet in elevation, only to climb back up. Red Mountain looms

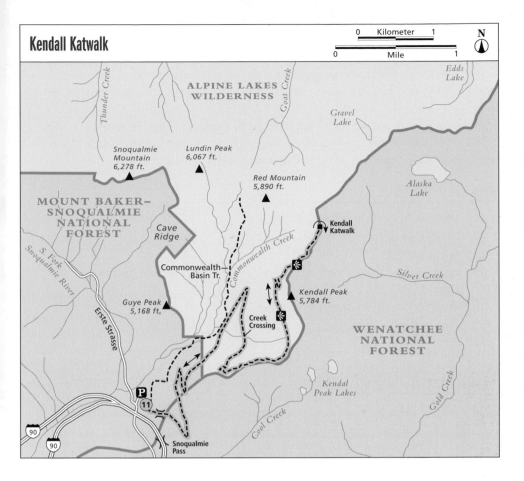

at the end of the Commonwealth Valley, Mount Rainier in the distant south. The trail skirts the south flank of Kendall Peak in an area called the Kendall Gardens. Here a lush mixture of Indian paintbrush, scarlet columbine, yarrow, and monkshood bloom among lady ferns. Above the gardens, the talus and cliff faces of Kendall Peak provide a home for marmots and garter snakes. Other flowers along the trail include phlox, lupine, Columbia lilies, penstemon, bleeding heart, queen's cup, monkey flowers, and thimbleberries.

Several patches of snow can cover the ridge south of the Katwalk into early August. The ridge leads to a flat area with sitting stones just below the Katwalk. You can sit here and look out over the Commonwealth Basin and the peaks that surround it. The iron-rich rock of the Red Mountain sits on a throne at the end of the valley, in stark contrast to the white rock and deep green trees of neighboring Snoqualmie Mountain to the west. Take a few steps around the corner and onto the Katwalk for a different set of views. Alta Mountain, Rampart Ridge, Kendall Peak, Chikamin Ridge, the top of Mount Stuart, Hibox Mountain, and a variety of other peaks and high points rise in the distance.

Note: This trail is easily accessed from Seattle, is the PCT, and delivers big views, so it gets crowded. Be prepared. And remember, not every hiker is excited to see dogs here—lots of trail reports complain about poop on the trail and out-of-control dogs. Remember you are an ambassador for all of us who want to take our dogs on the trails.

Option: If you and your pup still have gas in the tank, continue about 2.0 miles from the Katwalk to the lovely Gravel Lake (north of the trail) below Alaska Mountain for a plunge. There are good campsites here about as well.

Miles and Directions

0.0	Start from the Pacific Crest Trail parking lot.
0.2	Cross a creek on a wooden bridge.
3.4	Cross a creek.
5.0	Reach an alpine meadow below Kendall Peak. Mount Rainier comes into view to the south.
6.0	Reach the Katwalk. Return the way you came.
12.0	Arrive back at the parking lot.

BIRTHPLACE OF A GLACIER

Commonwealth Basin, the deep valley to the west below this section of the Pacific Coast Trail, was the birthplace of one of the glaciers that carved the valley through which I-90 now runs. The other glacier originated atop Source Lake. The two glaciers merged just south of Guye Peak and then split off, one portion heading into present-day Kittitas County and carving the Yakima River valley to the east and the other carving out the South Fork Snoqualmie River valley to the west.

12 Gothic Basin

This narrow basin of dark, naked rock, little pools, and a deep lake is wedged between the towers and buttresses of two formidable mountains. The trail is steep and rough, but it traverses beautiful forests high above the headwaters of the Sauk River. The uphill grunt ends when the trail crosses a pass into the awe-inspiring basin. The towering peaks and otherworldly rock make Gothic Basin an unforgettable destination. But this is not a hike for beginners or dogs not used to the rigors of the trail. Snow bridges in the early summer can be difficult for a dog to cross, especially on the return trip when your pup is tired.

Distance: 9.4 miles out and back

Hiking time: About 4.5 hours

Difficulty: Difficult due to steep, rocky terrain

Trail surface: Dirt and rock trail

Best season: Aug–Oct

Other trail users: None

Canine compatibility: Dogs must be leashed when in or around developed recreation sites, trailheads, interpretive trails, or campgrounds; voice control allowed in forest and wilderness areas. Always check at the trailhead for specific information regarding leash vs. voice control regulations.

Fees and permits: Northwest Forest Pass required to park at trailhead

Schedule: Open 24/7

Maps: USGS Monte Cristo, Bedal; Green Trails No. 143: Monte Cristo; Darrington Ranger District map, available at Verlot Public Service Center

Trail contact: Verlot Public Service Center, USDA Forest Service; (360) 691-7791; www.fs.usda.gov/mbs

Special considerations: This hike gains 2,900 feet of elevation, so you and your dog should be in good hiking shape before attempting.

Finding the trailhead: From Granite Falls go east on the Mountain Loop Highway for 30 miles. At Barlow Pass, park on the shoulder on the right side of the road or the parking lot to the left. The trail begins at the gated dirt road on the right (south) side of the highway. GPS: N48 30.91' / W121 26.65'

The Hike

Chiseled spires loom high above a deep frozen lake that seldom melts. Pikas signal to one another with high-pitched calls, and marmots sniff the alpine breeze from dark rocky towers. Gothic Basin awaits. This narrow, glacier-scraped basin sits between the three towers of Gothic Peak on one side and the equally jagged Del Campo Peak on the other. The year-round snowfield on Gothic Pass melts into Foggy Lake—a deep, fishless alpine lake beneath the peaks. A small stream flows out of the lake, pooling up in several ponds in the basin before plummeting steeply down the slope to Weden Creek.

It's easy to imagine that Gothic Basin got its name because the rugged terrain and steep peaks resemble gothic architecture. But it was actually named for William Gothic, an early prospector in the Monte Cristo area. The Monte Cristo townsite, which is just a few miles below Gothic Basin on the South Fork of the Sauk River,

The three summits of Gothic Peak rise above Foggy Lake. OLIVER LAZENBY

was home to 2,000 people at its peak in the 1890s. It was a base for miners, who extracted millions of dollars' worth of gold and silver from the mountains. Now it's one of Washington State's best ghost towns.

Don't underestimate the difficulty or length of the trail—2,900 feet of elevation in 4.7 miles may not sound excessive, but only the first 1.0 mile or so is on a flat road; the rest of the distance is brutally steep. You'll be climbing tight switchbacks that start out as firm, tacky dirt. Later on, the trail begins to resemble a creekbed. In the final 1.0 mile, angular rocks slices through the U-shaped, boulder-strewn trail.

Start out by walking past the gate at the Monte Cristo Road at Barlow Pass. The flat road runs parallel to the Sauk River for 1.0 mile. This is easy walking, with occasional views of the river. Several old mining trails take off to the right of the road, relics of a time when men and mules carried gold off the mountain. Stay on the road until it ends and a trail begins winding uphill. Soon you will reach a privy and a junction where you can go left to the Monte Cristo townsite or right for Gothic Basin.

After this junction the climb begins and doesn't let up. The trail winds through dense Douglas fir, cedar, spruce, and hemlock. Breaks in the trees show an occasional glimpse of Sheep Mountain, but views are rare. There's a brief break from climbing 3.0 miles from the trailhead, but your legs don't get much of a rest as you lumber across steep terrain, creeks, talus, and early-season snowfields. Even when conditions

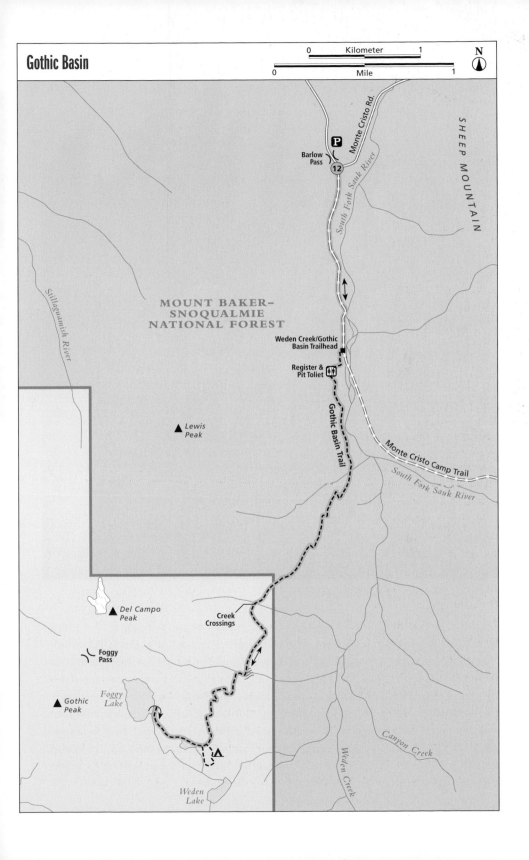

Gothic Basin

0 Kilometer 1
0 Mile 1

N

Monte Cristo Rd.

SHEEP MOUNTAIN

P
Barlow
Pass
12

South Fork Sauk River

MOUNT BAKER–
SNOQUALMIE
NATIONAL FOREST

Weden Creek/Gothic
Basin Trailhead

Register &
Pit Toliet

Stillaguamish River

▲ Lewis
   Peak

Gothic Basin Trail

Monte Cristo Camp Trail

South Fork Sauk River

▲ Del Campo
   Peak

Creek
Crossings

⌣ Foggy
   Pass

▲ Gothic
   Peak

Foggy
Lake

⌂

Weden Creek

Canyon Creek

Weden
Lake

A leashed hike through a field of wildflowers

are good, sections of loose trail and large boulders can be challenging. At 3.6 miles a waterfall splashes down several rocky steps. There are rumors of a mine shaft nearby.

After contouring across this hill, you will resume climbing. This final climb to the basin isn't as steep as the section below the falls, but the trail surface is worse. V-shaped ditches of jagged rock and boulders make up parts of the trail, and you'll need to use all four limbs in a few places. Just when you think your legs can't handle any more, you are forced to maneuver underneath several big fallen trees. This is especially grueling with an overnight pack. Finally the trail enters a notch and the dark, rocky basin spreads out in front of you. You reach this notch in just over 4.0 miles, but it's another 0.5 mile of steep scrambling before you reach the outlet of Foggy Lake.

From the notch, a couple campsites are wedged between trees to the left (south). Several more are at the outlet of the lake and at the lake itself. From Foggy Lake, a trail toward Del Campo Peak leads to a viewpoint to the east, where you can see Silvertip Peak, Foggy Peak, and Sheep Mountain. The peaks above Foggy Lake are popular with climbers, who scramble up all sides.

Miles and Directions

0.0   Start down the gated gravel road from the parking lot at Barlow Pass.

0.7   Pass several old mining trails on your right.

1.2   Pass a privy and start on the Gothic Basin/Weden Creek Trail; pass a self-registration box.

3.0   Cross through an avalanche gully and past several streams.

3.6   Cross a stream just below a scenic waterfall.

4.3   Pass through a notch and into Gothic Basin.

4.7   Reach Foggy Lake, at the top of Gothic Basin. Return the way you came.

9.4   Arrive back at the trailhead and parking lot at Barlow Pass.

MONTE CRISTO TOWNSITE

For a side trip after hiking to Gothic Basin, go south at the junction with the Gothic Basin/ Weden Creek trailhead near the South Fork Sauk and hike about 3.0 miles to the Monte Cristo townsite. The town was established in the late 1880s after Joseph Pearsall found samples of silver and gold in the Sauk River. Pearsall and his friend Frank Peabody, along with two investors, named the town Monte Cristo because they hoped it would make them as rich as the Count of Monte Cristo.

The area did prove to be rich in silver and gold. It produced millions of dollars in gold and silver ore, and the scale of the mining soon outgrew the power of human backs. By 1892 an investment company backed by John D. Rockefeller had bought most of the mines and built a railway—the Everett and Monte Cristo Railway—into the townsite.

Floods frequently damaged the railroad, which followed the turbulent South Fork Still- aguamish River through Lower Robe Canyon. By 1899 profit from the mines was declining and the railroad repairs were sucking up the investors' money. Rockefeller decided to rebuild and then sell the railroad, and Northern Pacific took over in 1903.

Soon after, when mining operations for silver and gold were no longer profitable, Monte Cristo became a resort for hunters, hikers, and other outdoor enthusiasts. Business dwin- dled, and by 1933 Monte Cristo was a ghost town. Today all that's left of the residences, shops, stables, churches, and infrastructure of Monte Cristo is a railroad turntable and a couple of neglected structures.

13 Lake Twenty-two

Lake Twenty-two has a well-justified reputation for being the most popular trail in the Stillaguamish Valley. It's loved by all kinds of hikers, from families with small children and dogs through mountaineers, because of its accessibility. Because of this heavy use, the trail shows constant evidence of being upgraded with new switchbacks, water bars, and boardwalks—especially around the lake perimeter. Clearly, what makes this hike exciting is the nice forest, high quality of boardwalks, and the ability to walk all the way around Lake Twenty-two and stare up the steep walls composing the basin.

Distance: 5.4 miles out and back, with optional 1.3-mile walk around the lake
Hiking time: 4–5 hours
Difficulty: Moderate due to steepness of the trail
Trail surface: Forested path, boardwalk; rocky
Best season: Summer and fall
Other trail users: None
Canine compatibility: Dogs must be leashed when in or around developed recreation sites, trailheads, interpretive trails, or campgrounds; voice control allowed in forest and wilderness areas. Always check at the trailhead for specific information regarding leash vs. voice control regulations. This is a very popular hike, and you may pass lots of other dogs, so unless your pooch is under strict voice control, consider using a leash.

Fees and permit: Northwest Forest Pass required
Schedule: Open 24/7
Maps: Green Trails No. 109: Granite Falls and No. 110: Silverton; USGS Verlot; USDAFS Mount Baker–Snoqualmie National Forest, Alpine Lakes Wilderness; *DeLorme: Washington Atlas and Gazetteer:* Page 96 D-2
Trail contacts: USDA Forest Service Darrington Ranger District, 1405 Emens St., Darrington 98241; (360) 436-1155; www.fs.fed.us/r6/mbs/about/drd.shtml. USDA Forest Service Verlot Public Service Center, 33515 Mountain Loop Hwy., Granite Falls 98252; (360) 691-7791.
Special considerations: No potable water at trailhead or on trail, so make sure you bring enough for you and your dog to last the entire day.

Finding the trailhead: From Seattle take I-5 north through Everett to exit 194 east (US 2). At the eastern end of the Hewlett Avenue trestle, follow signs directing you to WA 204 and Lake Stevens. The high volume of subdivision development in the Lake Stevens area, which services Everett, will undoubtedly lead to widening roads and additional stoplights along with increased traffic and eliminate current landmarks, so it is best to follow directions and highway signs.

Where WA 204 meets WA 9, turn left (north). At WA 92 turn right (east) and proceed to Granite Falls. Follow East Stanley Street through downtown Granite Falls to South Alder. Turn left (north). Pass Granite Falls Junior and Senior High Schools. At the stop sign, South Alder becomes the Mountain Loop Highway (WA 92).

Pass Granite Falls (the waterfall) in 1.4 miles; cross the South Fork Stillaguamish and continue upstream. In 11 miles east from the town of Granite Falls reach the USDA Forest Service Verlot Public Service Center on the north side of WA 92. In another 2.2 miles reach the trailhead for Lake Twenty-two. Turn right (south) and proceed 0.1 mile to the trailhead parking lot. On heavy-use days you will see cars parked on both sides of this short access road and also along WA 92. GPS: N48 04.62' / W121 44.75'

Lake Twenty-two PETER STEKEL

The Hike

Find the trailhead 50 feet west of the toilet. Walk 100 feet and come to a trail register kiosk and, 20 feet after that, a sign announcing the Lake Twenty-two Research Natural Area (RNA), established January 14, 1947. The big trees you see along the way predate any legal, scientific, or educational RNA protection.

Parents with very small children may elect to go no farther than here, since they will still enjoy a gravel path accompanied by a gurgling creek. The Mountain Loop Highway is close and all but invisible through a deep and shady forest.

Choosing to go on, soon cross a creek on a new bridge. The trail starts to climb on switchbacks that won't end until you reach the lake. There was a time when Lake Twenty-two epitomized a place overused and loved to death. The trail was beaten down and eroded. Several years of labor have cured most of that past misuse. Help minimize our impact in this beautiful forest; resist the temptation to cut switchbacks and step off any boardwalks that span damp ground.

Throughout its climb to Lake Twenty-two, the trail crosses many places where moisture is weeping out of the rocks. In season, these are perfect places to find wildflowers, and the soil remains moist throughout summer.

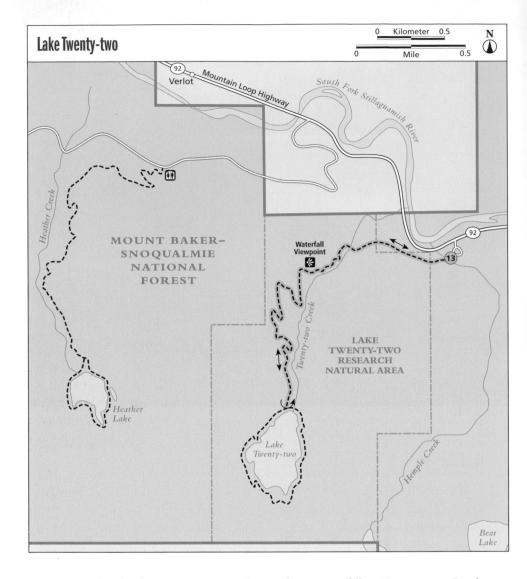

In 0.8 mile take the opportunity to admire a large waterfall on Twenty-two Creek. Reach a talus slope and leave the forest behind. On hot and sunny summer days, this section of trail has hikers yearning for shade. Nevertheless, it's excellent habitat for wildflowers, pikas, and birds, so keep your eyes open! Views up or across the Stillaguamish Valley to jagged mountain peaks are impressive.

Ducking back into the forest, the trail begins its final climb in shade to Lake Twenty-two. You know when you're almost there when the trail drops alongside the outflow creek. Views upward toward the lake reveal massive cliffs leading to Mount Pilchuck's summit. At the lake you're greeted by a long bridge spanning Twenty-two Creek and an even longer boardwalk. It's possible to circumnavigate the lake in either direction—your choice—for an additional 1.3 miles.

Great views from a bridge over the lake's outlet PETER STEKEL

Lunch spots and views abound. So do damp areas—be careful where you step and sit. Camping or open fires are prohibited at the lake. Due to its popularity, Lake Twenty-two is a perfect place to remember your outdoor manners. Pick up after yourself and leave no trash—including lunch leftovers. The food is not only bad for the critters and birds but also presents an unsightly mess for the next person who chooses to eat lunch in the same spot.

Miles and Directions

- **0.0** Start at the trailhead along WA 92.
- **0.8** Enjoy a waterfall view.
- **2.7** Reach Lake Twenty-two. Return the way you came. *Option:* Add 1.3 miles to your hike by walking around the lake.
- **5.4** Arrive back at the trailhead.

RESEARCH NATURAL AREA

The Lake Twenty-two Trail passes through a research natural area (RNA), public land established primarily for scientific and educational purposes under the Organic Administration Act of 1897. Principally located within national forests, RNAs exemplify typical or unique vegetation, geological, or aquatic features and preserve representative samples of ecological communities.

14 Boulder River–Feature Show Falls

The 259-foot Feature Show Falls splits into two streams midway through its perilous descent down the gorge wall of Boulder River Canyon, showering Boulder Creek below with a constant and always refreshing spray. If it's a warm summer day, you won't be alone—the falls is a popular place to cool off. Boulder Falls, a much smaller and less dramatic cascade, is viewable from the main trail 0.25 mile beyond the turn-off for Feature Show Falls.

Distance: 3.0 miles out and back
Hiking time: 1-2 hours
Difficulty: Easy to moderate
Trail surface: Dirt trail with lots of tree roots
Best season: Summer
Other trail users: Possibly a few mountain bikers
Canine compatibility: Dogs must be leashed when in or around developed recreation sites, trailheads, interpretive trails, or campgrounds; voice control allowed in forest and wilderness areas. Always check at the trailhead for specific information regarding leash vs. voice control regulations.
Fees and permits: Northwest Forest Pass required
Schedule: Open 24/7
Maps: USGS Mount Higgins, Meadow Mountain; *DeLorme: Washington Atlas & Gazetteer:* Page 32 C-5
Trail contact: Mount Baker-Snoqualmie National Forest, Darrington Ranger District; (360) 436-1155; www.fs.usda.gov/mbs
Special considerations: None

Finding the trailhead: Drive east from Arlington on WA 530 (the Mountain Loop Highway) for 19 miles and then turn right (south) onto French Creek Road (also known as FR 2010) and follow it for 4.5 miles until it ends at a large parking area and the trailhead for Boulder River Trail #734. GPS: N48 15.051' / W121 49.121'

The Hike

At the trailhead there is a small sign that says "Trail" and then 50 feet farther a kiosk with a "Boulder River Trail #734" sign, a small topo map showing where the trail goes, and a register for hikers/campers. (*Note:* There are no restrooms or privies at the parking area or along the hike.) The 5-foot-wide dirt trail is obviously well used but well maintained, with no litter in sight despite its popularity. The abundant second-growth forest tree canopy keeps the trail well shaded in the sun and relatively dry in the rain.

The trail continues along over a couple of small wooden footbridges over seasonal creeks that feed the rushing Boulder River down and to the right. Take a peek down at the river gorge by an old-growth cedar stump that serves as a nurse log for another smaller live tree, and then the trail turns left (south) and begins an uphill push. After another 0.1 mile up, the main trail turns left (south) and a side trail goes off to the right for 200 feet to the top of a small forested butte with peekaboo views past old-growth trees over the Boulder River's gorge.

Feature Show Falls RODDY SCHEER

Another view of beautiful Feature Show Falls RODDY SCHEER

Back on the main trail, pass a sign that marks where the trail crosses into the "Boulder River Wilderness," the wilderness area within the Mount Baker–Snoqualmie National Forest that is home to Feature Show Falls. ("Wilderness" means leave-no-trace rules are in effect, so make sure to bring your poop bags on this hike; it's hard to find easy spots for burying scat 200 feet from the river through this section.) Soon the Boulder River comes into view down and to the right, accompanied by the first sounds of rushing water. Moss-festooned bigleaf maple trees dapple the trail in green light. After another 0.25 of hiking, take an obvious side trail to the right (south) that leads down to an embankment with a picture-perfect view of Feature Show Falls and then down farther to the river at the base of the falls.

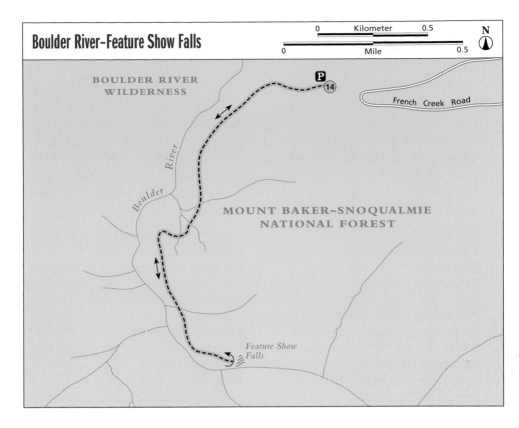

On a hot day, splashing around in the river at the base of the falls is a great way to cool off. After admiring Feature Show Falls, work your way back up the side trail and then turn right (east) to continue on the main trail for another 0.25 mile to see Boulder Falls, a smaller and much less dramatic cascade upstream from Feature Show Falls. Retrace your steps along the main trail to return to the trailhead.

Miles and Directions

0.0 Start at the trailhead kiosk marked with "Boulder River Trail #734," topo map of area, and trail register.

0.6 Look for an old-growth cedar stump and turnout with a view of Boulder River below.

0.7 Keep left at a fork where a side trail leads right to three backcountry campsites; in another 250 feet look for a sign on the right-hand side of the trail marking the border to the "Boulder River Wilderness."

1.0 First views of the Boulder River start to show up through the trees down and to the right of the trail.

1.25 Take a side trail to the right that leads down to the Boulder River and base of Feature Show Falls. Return to the main trail and continue heading east.

1.5 Arrive at a view of Boulder Falls from the main trail. Retrace your route on the main trail.

3.0 Arrive back at the trailhead.

15 Robe Canyon Historic Park–Lime Kiln Trail

Part of the Lime Kiln Trail follows the old Everett–Monte Cristo Railroad (built 1892–93 and abandoned 1933), which was used to haul timber from the forests upstream, copper ore from the Wayside Mine, and silver and gold from the town of Monte Cristo. In 1936 the tracks were pulled up and sold to companies in Japan for scrap. At trail's end you wind up at a rock-and-mortar limekiln. It was built circa 1900 to provide anhydrous lime from a nearby limestone quarry, which was used as a whitening agent at the Lowell paper mill. The lime was also used as a flux agent, helping in the process of melting ore for smelters in Everett.

Distance: 7.0 miles out and back
Hiking time: About 4 hours
Difficulty: Easy
Trail surface: Forested path, historic railroad grade
Best season: Spring through fall; best wildflowers Apr–May
Other trail users: Trail runners, equestrians
Canine compatibility: Leashed dogs permitted
Fees and permits: Northwest Forest Pass required
Schedule: Open 24/7
Maps: USGS Granite Falls; Green Trails #109: Granite Falls; USDAFS Mount Baker-

Snoqualmie National Forest; *DeLorme: Washington Atlas & Gazetteer.* Page 57 E-7
Trail contact: Snohomish County Department of Parks and Recreation; (425) 388-6600; www.snohomishcountywa.gov/200/Parks-Recreation
Special considerations: No toilet at trailhead. No potable water at trailhead or on trail. Stinging nettle and devil's club. Stillaguamish River is cold and swift with dangerous rapids and is not suitable for swimming, either for you or your pet.

Finding the trailhead: From the town of Granite Falls on WA 92, turn right onto S. Alder Avenue. Turn left at a T intersection onto E. Pioneer Street (becomes Menzel Lake Road). In about 1 mile turn left onto Waite Mill Road. Follow this for a short distance; after passing a school bus turnaround, bear left at the Y and follow a short gravel road uphill to the trailhead and parking lot for Robe Canyon Historic Park. GPS: N48 04.640' / W121 55.932'

The Hike

At the reader board beside the trailhead, study up on the history of the Everett–Monte Cristo Railroad. Begin the hike in a nice Douglas fir and western hemlock forest with a healthy understory of sword fern. Judging by the occasional tree stumps viewed through the thick second-growth woods, this used to be a forest of giants. No longer. On the other hand, the bigleaf maples are of truly impressive size.

After 0.2 mile the trail enters private property for the next 0.6 mile. Please stay on the trail. Red alder is common along this stretch of trail; so is hazelnut. In every wet spot it seems are the bright yellow flowers and shiny green leaves of western buttercup.

The Lime Kiln Trail provides wildflower lovers access to a portion of the historic Everett–Monte Cristo Railroad—abandoned since 1933. PETER STEKEL

In 0.7 mile come to a trail junction and turn right (east). The left fork is blocked off.

At 1.0 mile the trail splits; turn left (east) here, following the sign to Robe Canyon Park and Lime Kiln. At 1.2 miles enter Robe Canyon Historic Park, and at 1.4 miles cross Hubbard Creek on a substantial bridge. Quickly come to another trail junction and turn left (west) where a sign informs you that only hikers may proceed past this point. Those on horseback must turn around.

The trail now begins to drop steeply, and the understory of sword fern and hazelnut, which has been absent for nearly a mile, returns. Far below can be heard the roar of the South Fork Stillaguamish River. Seeps along the uphill side of the trail are perfect for finding bleeding heart and fringe-cup. If solely judged by its name, the latter wild-flower disappoints. In spring, both species remain common blooms all the rest of the way.

Bleeding heart (Dicentra formosa)
PETER STEKEL

Historic artifacts from the limekiln PETER STEKEL

After 1.9 miles comes a sidehill bridge over a portion of the hillside that has slid away. There is also a nice view of the river down below, wide and placid in this one spot. Kayakers affectionately call the river the "Stilly" and prize it for its challenging—some say dangerous—whitewater. Nowhere along this stretch of river is it safe to swim, as the water is swift, cold, and dangerous. You are now traversing the old Monte Cristo Railroad grade.

In short order, cross a log bridge (with convenient handrail) and then another sidehill bridge.

Reach Cutoff Junction in 2.5 miles. Don't be disappointed because there is no cutoff trail here. It appears to be a place-name, but the meaning is not clear. After hiking 3.0 miles you reach the limekiln, a bulky stone-and-brick structure (note the lack of mortar between the stones) standing about 25 feet tall and covered with epiphytic ferns.

From here the trail continues in a fairly level 0.8-mile loop to the river with a short side trail dropping steeply to the water. This is an ideal place for a picnic lunch beside the Stilly. Keep in mind that just below and around the corner is an impressive river-wide rapid. It is wise to ignore the large, deep, inviting pool at your feet and remain on dry land. From here, turn around and retrace your route to the trailhead and parking lot.

Robe Canyon Historic Park–Lime Kiln Trail

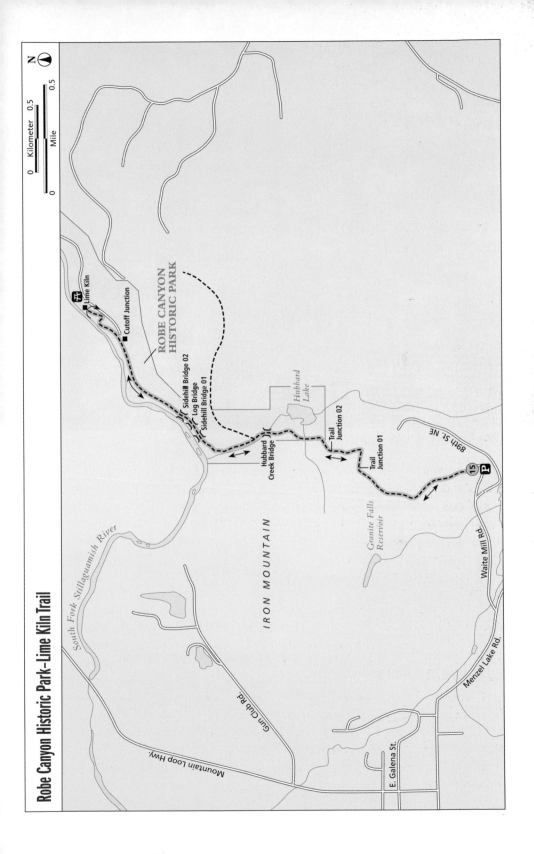

A hiker crosses the creek amid springtime flowers. PETER STEKEL

Miles and Directions

0.0 Start at the Robe Canyon Historic Park Trailhead and parking lot.

0.2 Enter private property.

0.7 Trail junction; turn right (east).

0.8 Leave private property.

1.0 Turn left (east) at the Robe Canyon Park and Lime Kiln sign.

1.9 Cross a sidehill bridge.

2.5 Reach Cutoff Junction.

3.0 Arrive at the limekiln.

3.5 Reach the South Fork Stillaguamish River. Retrace your route to the trailhead.

7.0 Arrive back at the trailhead and parking lot.

16 Deception Pass State Park–Goose Rock

At 484 feet, Goose Rock, in Deception Pass State Park, is the highest point on Whidbey Island. And Deception Pass is also considered Washington's most popular state park. Is it any wonder? The park offers three campgrounds, the Cornet Bay Retreat Center, and 3 miles of bike trails, 6 miles of horse trails, and 38 miles of hiking trails with 77,000 feet of saltwater shoreline. There are three sizable lakes, sand dunes, and dynamite views of Puget Sound. For plant lovers there is an old-growth forest and rhododendrons—all on 4,134 acres. The only thing marring this perfect place is the intermittent and unannounced flyovers by US Navy jets from nearby Whidbey Island Naval Air Station.

Distance: 6.1-mile double loop
Hiking time: 4–5 hours
Difficulty: Easy to moderate
Trail surface: Sand dune, forested path, asphalt, roadway
Best season: Year round; best wildflowers Mar–June
Other trail users: Trail runners
Canine compatibility: Leashed dogs permitted
Fees and permits: Discover Pass required
Schedule: Park open 6:30 a.m. to dusk, Apr through Sept; 8 a.m. to dusk, Oct through Mar
Maps: Green Trails No. 415: Deception Pass; USGS Deception Pass; *DeLorme: Washington Atlas & Gazetteer:* Page 55 A-9

Trail contacts: Deception Pass State Park: parks.state.wa.us/497/Deception-Pass. Deception Pass Park Foundation: www.deceptionpassfoundation.org.
Special considerations: Flush toilets, potable water, and picnic tables located at trailhead, North Beach, and Cranberry Lake at the park entrance. There is a fine for unleashed pets. Camping available within the park (reservations recommended). Restaurant, gas, and limited services at Seabolt's Smokehouse near park entrance.

Finding the trailhead: From the south, drive 20 miles on WA 20 from Coupeville to Deception Pass Road. Turn left (west) at the traffic signal. From the north, follow WA 20 from Burlington, crossing Fidalgo Island. After crossing the Deception Pass Bridge, drive 1 mile and turn right (west) at the traffic signal on Deception Pass Road. Drive west for 0.9 mile, passing the park's campgrounds, to the trailhead for West Beach. GPS: N48 23.971' / W122 39.844'

The Hike

Begin on the south side of the humongous West Beach parking area and pick up the trail beside the reader board and bicycle rack. Head out toward the food concession building and flush toilets on the right side of the asphalt Sand Dune Trail beside Cranberry Lake. Along the trail is the lovely blue-and-white seashore lupine.

At the head of this 1.2-mile loop trail is a short path that leads through the dunes to West Beach. The predominant plants here are American dune grass and a species of sedge, both of which stabilize the sand dunes.

Pacific rhododendron (Rhododendron macrophyllum) *on the Goose Rock Trail* PETER STEKEL

After enjoying this underappreciated community of sand dune plants, return through the forest along the other side of the loop. The forest contains Douglas fir, Sitka spruce, beach pine, and shrubs like salal and kinnikinnick.

Returning to the parking lot, head northward 0.2 mile and pick up the North Beach Trail for the main part of this hike. In 0.1 mile reach the campground amphitheater, pass through the parking lot, and pick up the trail again, which remains in the forest above gravelly and cobbled North Beach. There are some enormous Douglas firs along this stretch of trail along with Sitka spruce, red alder, western red cedar, and western hemlock.

In 0.5 mile come to a group picnic site with a large shelter. The trail goes through another parking lot here (toilets and water available) and continues on the other side to two new trails. Take the one signed "Bridge .2 / Goose Rock .4" and begin a moderately steep and exposed forested climb protected by a wooden guardrail.

After 0.3 mile of climbing, there is a parking lot above you on the right (south) and the trail passes under the Deception Pass Bridge (WA 20). Immediately find a sign with the disconcerting announcement that Goose Rock is *still* 0.4 mile away! Turn right (south) to follow this route. The trail climbs, sometimes steeply, and in 0.2 mile reaches a trail junction after first passing the James D. Endres Memorial Bench. Turn left (east) onto the NW Goose Rock Summit Trail. A hundred yards past that

Deception Pass State Park-Goose Rock

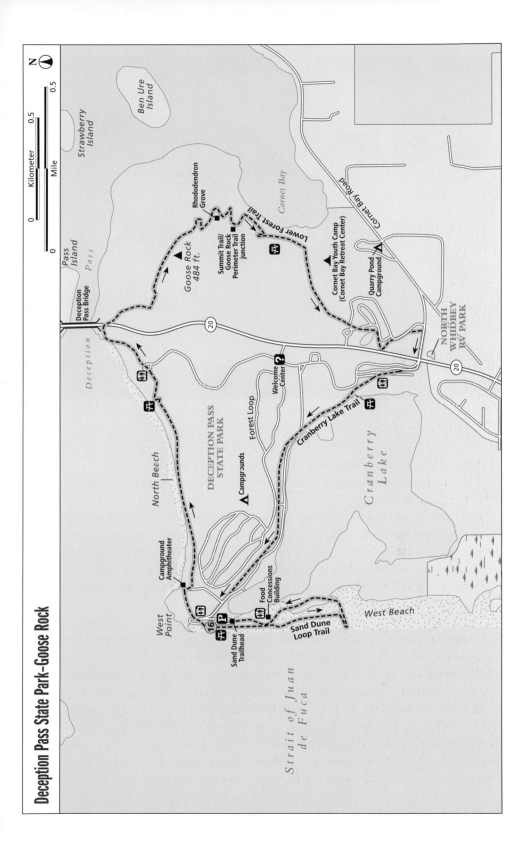

*Salal (*Gaultheria shallon*) in Deception Pass State Park* PETER STEKEL

comes another trail junction, this time with a well-defined waytrail. Keep going straight ahead to remain on route.

The last 0.2 mile to the summit is steep. Goose Rock is a bald hill scraped clean by glaciers 11,000 years ago.

Continue straight across the summit and the trail begins to switchback steeply down. The plants on this side of Goose Rock reflect its southern exposure. The forest is thinner, there isn't as much Methuselah's beard hanging from the trees, and there are several dry meadows and rocky outcrops. Toward the bottom of the hill, the forest regains its previous moister character. At 0.5 mile below the summit, enter a beautiful grove of Pacific rhododendron, Washington's state flower.

In another 0.3 mile reach a junction of the Summit Trail and the Goose Rock Perimeter Trail. Turn right (south) and in another 0.1 mile continue straight, onto the Lower Forest Trail. In 0.2 mile come to the restricted-access Cornet Bay Youth Camp (shown on maps as the Cornet Bay Retreat Center). The trail, now called the Discovery Trail, continues downhill for another 0.3 mile and reaches the Quarry Pond Campground. Walk 0.2 mile through the campground to Cornet Bay Road and follow this road another 0.2 mile to the traffic signal at WA 20.

Once safely across the highway, walk alongside the park entrance road, past the picnic area and welcome center. The road curves to the left; after 0.3 mile find the Cranberry Lake Trail. In another 0.3 mile cross the park road and pick up the trail, now called the West Beach Trail, on the other side. Follow this for 0.9 mile, always within shouting distance of the campground, to trail's end at the West Beach parking lot and trailhead.

Miles and Directions

0.0 Start at the West Beach parking lot and trailhead.

0.6 Complete the Sand Dune Loop Trail.

1.2 Arrive back at the parking lot.

1.4 Start at the trailhead for the North Beach Trail.

1.5 Come to a campground amphitheater; pass through the parking lot to regain the trail.

2.0 Reach the group picnic site and shelter and cross the North Beach parking lot.

2.1 Come to the Goose Rock Trailhead.

2.4 Pass under the Deception Pass Bridge (WA 20).

2.6 At the NW Goose Rock Summit Trail junction, turn left (east).

2.8 Reach the Goose Rock summit.

3.3 Pass through a rhododendron grove.

3.6 At the Summit Trail / Goose Rock Perimeter Trail junction, turn right (south).

3.7 Lower Forest Trail junction; continue straight.

3.9 Pass the Cornet Bay Youth Camp (Cornet Bay Retreat Center).

4.2 Walk through Quarry Pond Campground.

4.6 Cross at the traffic signal on WA 20 and walk along the park entrance road.

4.9 Pick up the Cranberry Lake Trail.

5.2 Cross the park road. The trail becomes the West Beach Trail.

6.1 Arrive back at trailhead and parking lot.

17 Marmot Pass

You may not hear the whistling of the Olympic Peninsula's endemic marmots from this high notch, but the view into the rugged heart of Olympic National Park won't let you down. Craggy basalt peaks—some of the hardest and sharpest in the Olympics—spread across the horizon on one side of the divide. In the other direction, the Pacific Ocean completes the panorama. While dogs are not allowed on most trails in Olympic National Park, this Upper Big Quilcene trail is in the Buckhorn Wilderness, just outside the park, where dogs are allowed.

Distance: 10.6 miles out and back

Hiking time: About 6 hours

Difficulty: Difficult due to length and elevation gain

Trail surface: Dirt trail

Best season: Mid-July–Oct

Other trail users: None

Canine compatibility: Dogs must be leashed when in or around developed recreation sites, trailheads, interpretive trails, or campgrounds; voice control allowed in forest and wilderness areas. Always check at the trailhead for specific information regarding leash vs. voice control regulations.

Fees and permits: Northwest Forest Pass required to park at trailhead

Schedule: Open 24/7

Map: Green Trails Custom Correct: Buckhorn Wilderness

Trail contact: USDA Forest Service, Quilcene Ranger District; (360) 765-2200

Special considerations: This hike includes an elevation gain of 3,450 feet, so make sure you and your dog are in good hiking shape.

Finding the trailhead: From Olympia drive 70 miles on US 101 North. About 1 mile south of Quilcene, turn left (west) onto Penny Creek Road. In 1.4 miles turn left onto Big Quilcene River Road. Continue on Big Quilcene River Road, bearing right in 3.1 miles. Reach FR 2750, 9.4 miles after turning onto Big Quilcene River Road. Follow this road up and down for 4.5 miles until you reach the parking area next to Big Quilcene Trail 833, 15.3 miles from US 101. GPS: N47 49.67' / W123 02.47'

The Hike

Marmot Pass is one of the prettiest alpine viewpoints in the Olympics. The Mount Constance and Warrior Peak group nearby are some of the tallest, craggiest peaks on the dry side of the Olympic Range, and an assortment of other peaks line the horizon. Several paths lead to this high pass. The classic route along the Big Quilcene River described here is the shortest. It leads through deep forests alongside misty pools and logjams in the river and up through flower-filled meadows past several campsites to a final push to a gap between mountains.

At the pass you can look back the way you came to view meadows and Puget Sound in the distance. Marmot Pass is near some of the tallest mountains in the Olympics. The peaks demonstrate the rain shadow effect of the western Olympic Mountains. Mount Constance, at 7,756, feet is barely lower than 7,979-foot-tall

Wildflowers and basalt crags on the way to Marmot Pass OLIVER LAZENBY

Mount Olympus, yet it has a fraction of the snow and glaciers. That's because Mount Olympus is directly west of Mount Constance and collects the storms blowing off the Pacific Ocean. Much less water and snow make it farther east to Mount Constance and the east side of the Olympics.

The trail begins deep in a mosaic of green surrounding the foaming Big Quilcene River. Big trees grow out of a low carpet of moss. The meandering trail occasionally nears the cool stream that plunges and pools between snarls of downed trees and mossy boulders. As the trail climbs, the low mat of understory moss is slowly joined by taller ground-cover plants like Oregon grape and salal.

Several small creeks flow from beneath barren basalt piles on the tall northern slopes and into the creek. The streamside zones are thick with berries and some patches of spiny devil's club. Elderberries and thimbleberries reach for the sun, and the moisture feeds salmonberries the size—and sometimes color—of strawberries.

The trail switches back at 1.7 miles and then switchbacks again shortly after and drops beneath a waterfall that fans out over volcanic rock. The trail begins climbing in earnest after the falls. The path climbs away from the creek and skirts beneath craggy rock spires on the southern slopes of Buckhorn and Iron Mountains. Small clumps of Alaskan yellow cedars and subalpine fir grow along the trail. A variety of

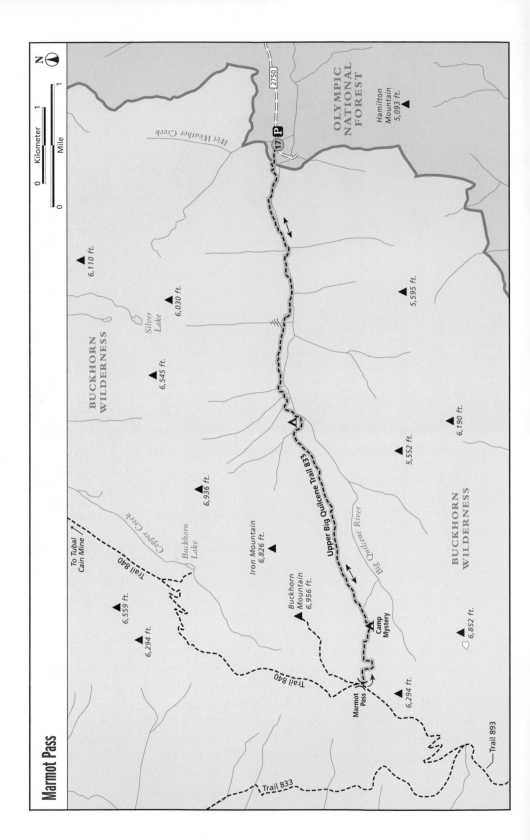

Marmot Pass

OLYMPIC NATIONAL FOREST

BUCKHORN WILDERNESS

BUCKHORN WILDERNESS

Wet Weather Creek

Silver Lake

Copper Creek

Buckhorn Lake

Big Quilcene River

Upper Big Quilcene Trail 833

To Tubal Cain Mine

Trail 840

Trail 840

Trail 833

Trail 893

Marmot Pass

Camp Mystery

Hamilton Mountain 5,093 ft.

Iron Mountain 6,826 ft.

Buckhorn Mountain 6,956 ft.

6,110 ft.

6,030 ft.

6,545 ft.

6,936 ft.

5,595 ft.

5,552 ft.

6,190 ft.

6,559 ft.

6,294 ft.

6,852 ft.

6,294 ft.

2750

P

17

N

0 Kilometer 1

0 Mile 1

Leashes are optional on the trail.

flowers sprout in talus crevices. Arnicas and asters add color to the dark mountains in the background. About a dozen wildflowers are endemic to the Olympic Peninsula, and at least a couple of them grow along the trail to Marmot Pass. Look for purple Piper's bellflower and Olympic violets. Smatterings of much more common Indian paintbrush, lupine, and Queen Anne's lace also grow in gardens along the trail.

The wildflowers keep getting better until you reach Camp Mystery, a flat spot with established camps near a creek at 5.0 miles. From here, hike up a few final switchbacks toward Marmot Pass. The view behind you swells all the time, until at last Puget Sound appears. Once you reach the crest of Marmot Pass, a whole new world of wilderness appears. Gaze west into the heart of Olympic National Park. Mount Mystery, Mount Deception, and a line of rugged points called The Needles crown the top of a tall ridge. Between Marmot Pass and this row of mountains, the headwaters of the Dungeness River drain a deep green gulf.

Miles and Directions

0.0   Start at the Upper Big Quilcene 833 Trailhead on FR 2750.

1.9   Pass a fan-shaped waterfall on the right side of the trail. Shortly after, cross another small stream; the trail begins climbing in earnest.

3.2   Pass several campsites along the Big Quilcene River.

5.0   Pass Camp Mystery—several campsites scattered around water trickling off snow near Marmot Pass.

5.3   Reach Marmot Pass. Dogs are not allowed past this point. Return the way you came.

10.6 Arrive back at the trailhead.

18 Spruce Railroad Trail

This fun singletrack trail runs along the shores of Lake Crescent in Olympic National Park. It's bounded by steep slate walls above and the water below. Check out a tiny "hole in the rock" tunnel, and after your workout, relax beside mountains reflecting in the turquoise lake.

Distance: 4.0 miles point to point
Hiking time: About 2 hours
Difficulty: Easy to moderate
Trail surface: Smooth dirt and gravel with some rocky areas. Most of the trail is 3 to 4 feet wide, although it has eroded to 2 feet and is banked toward the lake in places.
Best season: Year-round, but best May–Sept
Other trail users: Bicyclists, equestrians
Canine compatibility: Leashed dogs permitted

Fees and permits: No fees or permits required
Schedule: Open 24/7
Map: USGS Lake Crescent
Trail contact: Olympic National Park, 600 E. Park Ave., Port Angeles 98362; (360) 565-3130; www.nps.gov/olym
Special considerations: This trail is one of only a couple in Olympic National Park that allow dogs. Help protect this privilege by keeping your pet leashed and under close control.

Finding the trailhead: Take US 101 to a junction with East Beach Road at mile marker 232, just east of Lake Crescent. Follow this winding, paved road 3.2 miles, passing the Log Cabin Resort and turning left on another paved road bearing a sign for the Spruce Railroad Trail. This road crosses the Lyre River and reaches a parking area near some private residences. The trail begins from a sign on the west side of the road. GPS: N48 5.533' / W123 48.025' (east trailhead); N48 4.025' / W123 50.048' (west trailhead)

The Hike

This trail, one of only a couple in Olympic National Park that allow dogs, offers a gentle stroll along the north shore of Lake Crescent, making a point-to-point hike that is discussed here from east to west. It follows an old railbed that was built during World War I to transport Sitka spruce from the then-inaccessible western part of the peninsula to the aircraft factories. Sitka spruce has a superior ratio of strength to weight and was therefore coveted for the construction of biplane airframes. The railroad was completed in a remarkable time of only six weeks, but the war was over before the first logs rolled eastward on the rails. The railway was active through the 1950s, when it was abandoned and subsequently turned into a trail. It is one of the only trails in Olympic National Park where mountain bikes are permitted.

The trail begins by running inland from the North Shore Road, climbing gently to reach the old railroad grade. As the railbed runs southward, it passes through a mixed forest of red alder and Douglas fir, skirting inland to avoid private residences along the lakeshore. It then descends to the shoreline, although dense trees screen out views of the water. A rough spur path to Harrigan Point brings you to a grassy spit that offers the first unobstructed vistas of the hike.

A bridge crosses a small inlet along the Spruce Railroad Trail. NATALIE L. BARTLEY

A short distance farther, the main trail climbs a bit to round the rocky headland of Devils Point. An old tunnel was blasted through the bedrock of the point to accommodate the railway, but it has since been sealed off with rocky debris. The point itself offers fine views of the north arm of the lake and Mount Storm King rising above the waters to the south. Pacific madrones thrive in the thin soils of this sunny locale.

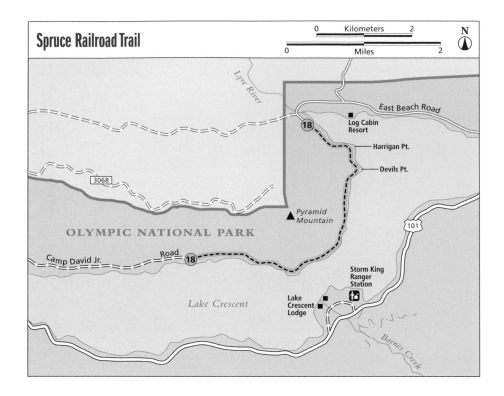

Kilometers

Miles

N

Lyre River

East Beach Road

18

Log Cabin Resort

Harrigan Pt.

Devils Pt.

3068

Pyramid Mountain

101

OLYMPIC NATIONAL PARK

Camp David Jr. Road

18

Storm King Ranger Station

Lake Crescent

Lake Crescent Lodge

Barnes Creek

A bridge soon arches above the waters of a narrow and rocky cove, and its turquoise depths have a gemlike clarity. The imposing rock faces that rise all around this inlet are the exposed foundation of Pyramid Peak.

Just beyond the bridge are fine views of the western arm of the lake, with the towering green wall of Aurora Ridge dominating its south shore. The next stretch of shoreline is frequently punctuated by openings where the trail skirts the base of sheer cliffs. Lake Crescent Lodge occupies the alluvial delta of Barnes Creek on the far side of the lake. A second tunnel is soon reached, and the eastern entrance of this one has not been blocked. The tunnel is choked with rubble and rotting timber, however, and exploring it would be an unsafe proposition. Old sections of rail are reminiscent of earlier times as the path makes its way through sun-dappled groves of red alder to reach the western trailhead. Just before arriving at the trailhead outhouse, the path departs from the railbed and drops to meet the end of Camp David Jr. Road.

Miles and Directions

0.0   Start at the east trailhead.

0.8   Take the spur to Harrigan Point.

1.1   Reach Devils Point.

2.9   Come to the second tunnel.

4.0   Arrive at the west trailhead.

19 Madison Creek Falls

Madison Creek Falls' 76-foot horsetail drop into a perfect woodland pool is an awe-inspiring scene; all the better that it is easily accessible via a relatively flat, paved, 250-foot trail through the forest at the base of Olympic National Park's wild and woolly Elwha River drainage.

Distance: 500 feet out and back
Hiking time: About 10 minutes
Difficulty: Easy
Trail surface: Paved
Best season: Year-round
Other trail users: None
Canine compatibility: Leashed dogs permitted
Fees and permits: Olympic National Park admission fee
Schedule: Open 24/7

Map: *DeLorme: Washington Atlas & Gazetteer:* Page 29 E-9
Trail contact: Olympic National Park, 600 E. Park Ave., Port Angeles 98362; www.nps.gov/olym; (360) 565-3130
Special considerations: This short trail is one of only a couple in Olympic National Park that allow dogs. Help protect this privilege by keeping your pet leashed and under close control.

Finding the trailhead: From its junction with US 101, about 8.5 miles west of Port Angeles, follow Olympic Hot Springs Road south for 2 miles to the Madison Falls parking area on the left (east). GPS: N48 02.467'/W123 35.394'

The Hike

This short trail is one of only a couple trails in Olympic National Park that allow dogs. Be sure to keep your pet leashed and under close control. Pick up the marked, paved trail by the small parking area and follow it as it winds into the side of the gorge and terminates at an overlook right below Madison Falls. Those interested in a closer look, or wanting to splash around in the spray, can venture into the pool at the bottom of the falls—but beware, glacial-fed Madison Creek is cold, even for your dog!

Miles and Directions

0.0 Start at the marked trailhead by the Madison Creek Falls parking lot off Olympic Hot Springs Road.

250' Arrive at the Madison Creek Falls overlook. Return the way you came.

500' Arrive back at the trailhead.

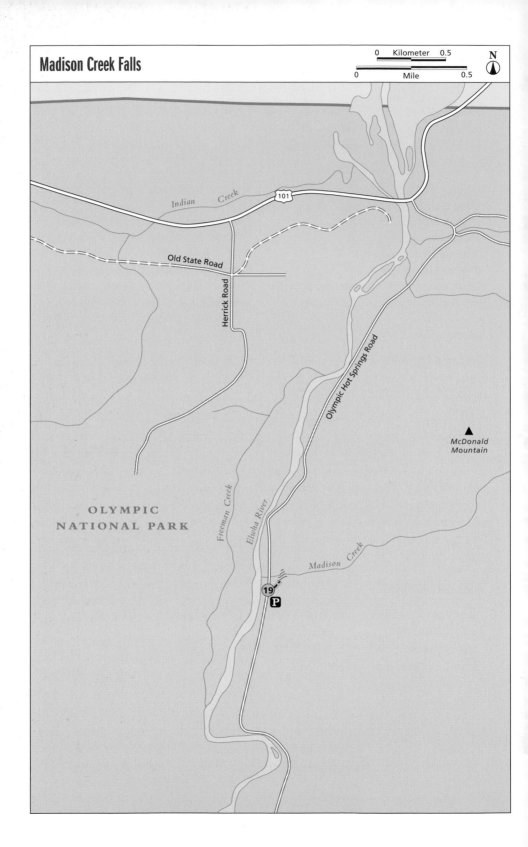

Madison Creek Falls

0 Kilometer 0.5
0 Mile 0.5

N

Indian Creek

101

Old State Road

Herrick Road

Olympic Hot Springs Road

McDonald
Mountain

OLYMPIC
NATIONAL PARK

Freeman Creek

Elwha River

Madison Creek

19
P

One of the most accessible of the Olympic Peninsula's cascades, Madison Falls tumbles 76 feet into a verdant gorge.

A RIVER REBORN: RESTORING THE ELWHA

Olympic National Park has been in the news a lot lately thanks to the largest dam-removal project in the history of the world along the Elwha River there, not far from Madison Falls. The massive undertaking to remove the two antiquated hydroelectric dams and restore a once-upon-a-time thriving wild riparian ecosystem along the Elwha started in 2011 and took three years to complete. According to members of the Lower Elwha Klallam Tribe, whose ancestors lived by the river for thousands of years, the Elwha was home to some of the healthiest salmon runs on the West Coast before the dams went in starting in 1910. Today scientists are amazed at how quickly the riparian environment is reverting to its former glory, even though the dams had been in place for more than a century. Salmon are migrating past the former dam sites, while trees and shrubs are putting down roots in the drained reservoir beds. It's an exciting time to visit the Elwha drainage if you are in the area anyway, so make sure to save some time to check out the former Elwha Dam view and access and former Lake Mills access sites.

20 Oyster Dome

Oyster Dome pokes its bald head above the beautiful lowland forests of the Chuckanut Range between Bellingham and the Skagit Valley. The view of the San Juan Islands and Samish Bay from Oyster Dome are incredible. The shimmering water is dotted with infinite islands. Some are just big enough for a seagull to take a nap on; others are as tall as Oyster Dome's summit. The best part? You can hike this beautiful trail year-round.

Distance: 6.2 miles out and back
Hiking time: About 3.5 hours
Difficulty: Moderate due to elevation gain and steep sections
Trail surface: Dirt trail
Best season: Year-round; more pleasant when it's dry
Other trail users: None
Canine compatibility: Leashed dogs permitted
Fees and permits: Discover Pass required to park at trailhead

Schedule: Open 24/7
Map: USGS Bow
Trail contact: Washington Department of Natural Resources, Northwest Region; (360) 856-3500; dnr.wa.gov
Special considerations: This hike includes an elevation gain of 1,800 feet, so you and your pet should be in good hiking shape before attempting.

Finding the trailhead: From Burlington drive 10 miles north on Chuckanut Drive (WA 11). The trailhead is on the right (east) between mileposts 10 and 11. Park on the shoulder across from the trailhead. From Bellingham travel 10 miles south on Chuckanut Drive to reach the trailhead. GPS: N48 36.49' / W121 25.99'

The Hike

Oyster Dome is a fantastic year-round hike in an interesting area of lowland mountains, lush forests, and tranquil lakes. With ample trails and viewpoints, the Chuckanut Mountains offer plenty of exploring. The hike to Oyster Dome is the most scenic hike in the area and a good sample of the coastal Chuckanut Mountains, which stretch from Bellingham to the Skagit Valley.

Blanchard Mountain, the mountain Oyster Dome is on, rises right out of the salt water. This makes for unparalleled views of islands and water. The shimmering sound is dotted with more islands than you can count—some are massive and mountainous; others are solitary points of rock just big enough to pull a canoe onto. To the southeast, the snowcapped Olympic Mountains cradle the shimmering water and provide a backdrop to the islands. From atop the bald dome, the Chuckanut Range stretches as far as you can see to the north, ending abruptly at the Skagit lowlands to the south.

Oyster Dome is slightly more than 2,000 feet above the water. The bare dome pokes out of a thick, moist second-growth forest with firs and cedars hiding the

Sandstone boulders and lush forest cover the Chuckanut Mountains OLIVER LAZENBY

The San Juan Islands from the top of Oyster Dome OLIVER LAZENBY

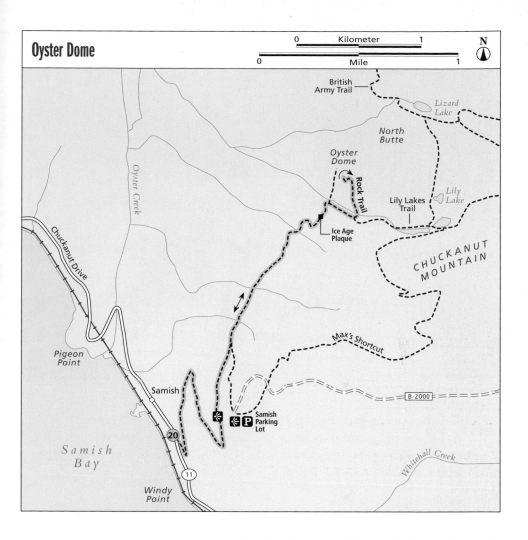

original forest's giant stumps. Snowberries, salal, sword fern, and vine maples make up the understory.

At the trailhead on Chuckanut Drive, you can breathe deeply of the salty air. Nearby Bellingham consistently ranks in the American Lung Association's list of cities with the cleanest air. The trail has a steep start and a steep finish, with some pleasant hiking on flatter ground in between. Get your fill of the salty sea breeze and warm your muscles by huffing up the switchbacks that start immediately on a wide, well-maintained trail. A quarter-mile later you will still be able to see Chuckanut Drive well below you. Just over 1.0 mile into the hike, trees are crowding into an old clear-cut where you get your first glimpse of the San Juan Islands and Puget Sound. A bench at 1.2 miles is a nice spot for a water break.

Soon you'll be meandering along the side of the hill on a relatively flat trail choked with jagged rocks, roots, and occasional little streams and patches of mud.

© ISTOCK.COM/BAWANCH

At 2.8 miles you reach an intersection. Go left to continue toward Oyster Dome. Lily Lake is to the right and makes a nice side trip. It's a calm lake surrounded by tall firs and cedars and is about 0.5 mile out of the way. The rest of the hike—about 0.3 mile—is brutally steep, but it pays off with breathtaking views.

Miles and Directions

- **0.0** Start at the Pacific Northwest Trailhead on Chuckanut Drive.
- **1.2** Reach a viewpoint with a bench.
- **1.6** Go left at the junction with the trail to the Samish Overlook parking lot.
- **2.8** Go left at the junction with the Lily Lakes Trail.
- **3.1** Reach the bare rock at the top of Oyster Dome. Return the way you came.
- **6.2** Arrive back at the trailhead.

21 Yellow Aster Butte

You'll see grand views and colorful flowers from every step of this trail, but the scenery peaks at the blueberry-covered summit. From here your eyes can wander the stunning naked cliffs of the American and Canadian Border Peaks, the glassy tarns in the meadow beneath the butte, or the icy masses of Mounts Baker and Shuksan. Thanks to its gentle grade and constant sensory stimulation, the trail to Yellow Aster Butte is one of the most pleasant hikes in the North Cascades.

Distance: 8.0 miles out and back
Hiking time: About 5 hours
Difficulty: Difficult due to elevation gain and sections of snowy trail
Trail surface: Dirt trail with patches of snow near the top
Best season: July–Oct
Other trail users: None
Canine compatibility: Dogs must be leashed when in or around developed recreation sites, trailheads, interpretive trails, or campgrounds; voice control allowed in forest and wilderness areas. Always check at the trailhead for specific information regarding leash vs. voice control regulations.

Fees and permits: Northwest Forest Pass required to park at trailhead
Schedule: Open 24/7
Maps: USGS Mount Larrabee; Green Trails No. 14: Mount Shuksan
Trail contact: Mount Baker Ranger District; (360) 856-5700; www.fs.usda.gov/mbs
Special considerations: No camping allowed on the trail; camp only in established sites at the lakes under the butte. This hike includes an elevation gain of 2,500 feet, so both you and your dog should be in good hiking shape before attempting.

Finding the trailhead: From Deming go east on the Mount Baker Highway (WA 542) 33 miles to FR 3065 (signed "Twin Lakes Road"). The road is behind the Department of Transportation's Shuksan maintenance facility. Continue north on FR 3065 for 4.3 miles until you reach the trailhead and a privy at a switchback. Parking is available on the road shoulder before and after the trailhead. GPS: N48 56.58' / W121 39.69'

The Hike

It's such a pleasure to hike near volcanoes. Views of Mount Baker, just 15 miles away, start less than 0.5 mile into this hike. Mount Shuksan, its neighbor to the east, soon joins it on the skyline, and the views only get better as you climb. The hike is 8.0 miles long, but those miles fly by thanks to stunning alpine scenery. The trail climbs continuously, but it never gets very steep. Maybe it's the refreshing berries along the way or the ample views and wildflowers, but the trail is a joy from start to finish.

As the name suggests, Yellow Aster Butte is surrounded by gardens of wildflowers. But you probably won't see yellow asters. Both purple asters and yellow daisies grow in clumps along the trail, so that's good enough. Yellow Aster Butte is home to

A steep path leads the final stretch to Yellow Aster Butte's summit. OLIVER LAZENBY

gorgeous color all year long, whether it's the array of wildflowers that fill the meadows near the top of the butte, the blueberry and mountain ash displaying brilliant wine-colored foliage in fall, or the white and blue tarns in different stages of thawing below the butte.

A lawn of blueberries and heather grow atop the butte. From this vantage, the most impressive peaks are Mounts Baker and Shuksan to the south; the bare cliff faces of the American Border Peak, the Canadian Border Peak, and Mount Larrabee to the north; and Goat Mountain to the southeast. Tomyhoi Peak is the complicated mass of rock to the northwest with the waterfall roaring through a narrow gap in its rocks. Tomyhoi is a favorite among climbers, who access the mountain from the Yellow Aster Butte Trail.

The best views are from the top of the butte, but the euphoria of endless beauty surrounds the trail. Many hikers never reach the top of Yellow Aster Butte because there is so much to see and explore along the way. This hike is entirely without boring sections—no long switchbacks without views, no flat marches with unchanging scenery.

A dense, low jungle of fireweed, false hellebore, thimbleberry, and cow parsnip blanket the lower slopes of Yellow Aster Butte. After kicking up dust onto the brushy flowers, you and your dog hike through a patchy forest of silver and Douglas firs. As the trail climbs, the trees shrink and you begin traverses through meadows of asters, lupines, scarlet columbines, Indian paintbrush, monkey flowers, and bear grass that are soon joined by heather and blueberries at higher elevations. Color explodes from the vegetation all season long. Two miles below the summit, you reach a junction with the trail to Tomyhoi Lake. It goes right, climbing Gold Run Pass before descending 1,500 feet to the big lake. The meadow surrounding this junction or, better yet, the top of Gold Run Pass makes an excellent place to stop for photos, snacks, or lunch.

The blueberries at Yellow Aster Butte are bountiful and tasty. They start in the meadow below Gold Run Pass, and you can find them near the trail from here to the very top of the butte, where in fall they color the round butte in a deep, dark scarlet.

At nearly 4.0 miles from the trailhead, the trail splits. The left path goes toward the tarn-filled meadow below the butte. Here you'll find reflective tarns surrounded by snow and even more berry bushes and wildflowers. Campsites are plentiful here. A walk toward the cone-shaped peak to the south or toward Tomyhoi Peak will reveal more and more places to pitch a tent. Stay on the trail, as wandering boots have stamped parts of the meadow into oblivion in recent years.

The final spur to the butte is steep and direct, but it's worth the sweat for the 360-degree views. An informal trail goes between here and the slightly higher point to the north, but it's a trail more suited to goats than humans.

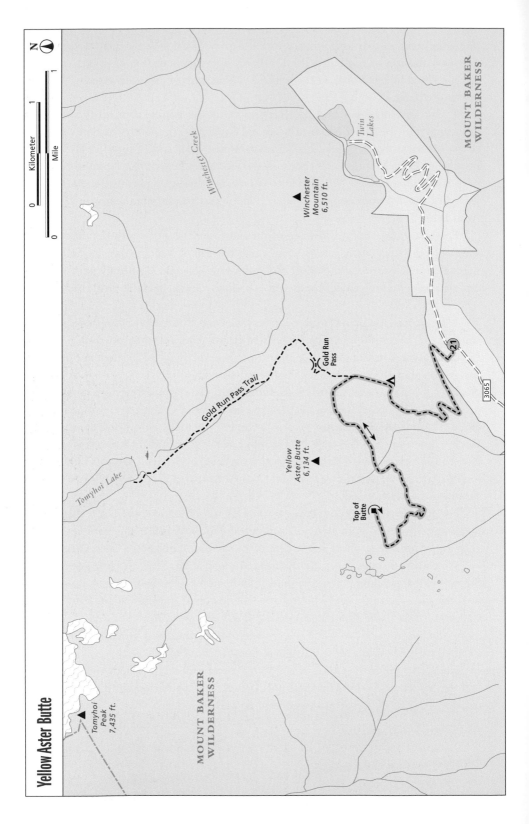

Yellow Aster Butte

MOUNT BAKER WILDERNESS

Tomyhoi Peak
7,435 ft.

Tomyhoi Lake

Gold Run Pass Trail

Yellow Aster Butte
6,134 ft.

Top of Butte

Gold Run Pass

Winchester Creek

Winchester Mountain
6,510 ft.

Twin Lakes

MOUNT BAKER WILDERNESS

21

3065

N

0   1   Kilometer
0   1   Mile

© ISTOCK.COM/PIERDELUNE

Miles and Directions

0.0 Start at the Yellow Aster Butte Trailhead off FR 3065. The trail starts behind a pit toilet at a bend in the road.

0.3 Views of Mount Baker begin.

1.5 Cross a boggy area and pass a campsite on the right.

1.9 Bear left at the junction with the Gold Run Pass Trail, which climbs up to Gold Run Pass and Tomyhoi Lake.

3.8 Turn right (north) for the final climb up the butte, or go left (southwest) to reach the campsites at the lakes below Yellow Aster Butte.

4.0 Reach the summit of Yellow Aster Butte. Return the way you came.

8.0 Arrive back at the trailhead.

22 Maple Pass Loop

This loop hike starts at the top of Rainy Pass, near some of the most iconic features on the North Cascades Highway. The loop trail circles Lake Ann, a beautiful glacier-carved tarn, on a high ridge speckled with larches, flowers, and blueberries. The views are dominated by the towering hulks of Frisco Mountain, Corteo Peak, and Black Peak. Beyond the emerald oval of Lake Ann, a golden ridge spreads out between Cutthroat Peak and Golden Horn.

Distance: 7.4-mile loop
Hiking time: About 4 hours
Difficulty: Moderate due to length and elevation gain
Trail surface: Dirt trail
Best season: Late July–Oct
Other trail users: None
Canine compatibility: Dogs must be leashed when in or around developed recreation sites, trailheads, interpretive trails, or campgrounds; voice control allowed in forest and wilderness areas. Always check at the trailhead for specific information regarding leash vs. voice control regulations.
Fees and permits: Northwest Forest Pass required to park at trailhead. Wilderness camping in North Cascades National Park requires a free permit. Permits are available at the Wilderness Information Center in Marblemount.
Schedule: Open 24/7
Maps: USGS Washington Pass, Mount Arriva; Green Trails No. 49: Mount Logan, No. 50: Washington Pass
Trail contact: Methow Valley Visitor Center, Okanogan-Wenatchee National Forest, 49 Hwy. 20, Winthrop 98862; (509) 996-4000
Special considerations: Camping is not allowed within 0.25 mile of Lake Ann, Maple Pass, or Heather Pass due to fragile meadows that have been trampled and are slowly revegetating. This hike includes an elevation gain of 2,100 feet, so hikers and their dogs need to be in good hiking shape.

Finding the trailhead: From Mazama go west on WA 20 (North Cascades Highway) for 21 miles to milepost 158, at the top of Rainy Pass (Rainy Pass is 69 miles west of Concrete). Turn left (south) into the Rainy Pass Picnic Area, following signs. GPS: N48 30.91' / W120 44.14'

The Hike

The North Cascades is the best place in the state to hike if you like being high in the mountains surrounded by glaciers, peaks, lakes, and naked rock. From the highway, the most iconic views are near Rainy Pass and Washington Pass. At these two high passes, you'll also find trailheads for some of the most spectacular and convenient hiking in the North Cascades. From a trailhead at the top of Rainy Pass, a relatively short loop hike to Heather and Maple Passes meanders through rugged terrain with brilliant fall colors and panoramic views.

Because of lingering snow and radiant autumn color, Maple Pass is a great fall destination. If you go at the right time in October, you can watch golden larches slowly shed their needles onto steep slopes of crimson blueberry and huckleberry foliage. To the north, a pointy peak called Golden Horn mimics the color of the autumn larches.

Lakes, meadows, flowers, high peaks, and the ability to hike in a loop make this trail an excellent hike anytime during the season. That season, however, isn't very long—the ridge between Heather and Maple Passes typically doesn't shed its snow until August.

Most people hike the loop in a counterclockwise direction—the more gradual ascent route, which is also more open and scenic. Start by hiking up the dirt trail from the parking lot. The paved Rainy Lake Trail, which goes left (south) from the trailhead, is the return path. The trail climbs gradually through big firs and mountain hemlocks, traversing the occasional slide path choked with alders beaten sideways and dusty thimbleberries and elderberries. A junction at 1.3 miles leads to Lake Ann, a refreshing lake in a deep bowl. Lake Ann is a popular destination and turnaround spot for many hikers and for tourists traveling over WA 20, and you'll shed some of the crowds as you get beyond the lake. The trail above Lake Ann on the talus slope to the north affords a beautiful vantage of the lake and its cute ovular island.

The trail continues up across steep, loose slopes through patchy blueberries. Spirea, Indian paintbrush, gentians, and columbines grow along the trail. The occasional mountain ash lends its leaves and berries to the fall color show.

You climb through a few short switchbacks above the lake before reaching Heather Pass. The surrounding peaks—Black and Corteo—come into view. Across the Granite Creek Valley (WA 20) is Whistler Mountain and Cutthroat Peak. Golden Horn seems to glow beyond them. Oddly enough, Golden Horn and everything northwest of Heather Pass are not part of North Cascades National Park. That includes the granite monoliths of the Liberty Bell, Concord Tower, Lexington Tower, and the Early Winter Spires—some of the most awe-inspiring and iconic peaks in the North Cascades (or anywhere else). Take solace in the fact that the land south of you is protected and that an effort is under way to expand the park.

From Heather Pass the trail is an airy ridge walk with spectacular views on both sides of the trail. Horns, knife edges, jagged peaks, crags—there aren't enough words to describe these mountains. The beauty of the North Cascades spreads out all around as you amble past numerous viewpoints and dips in the trail. At Maple Pass, larches frame Lake Ann and views stretch out to the east.

The descent toward Rainy Lake is steep. It begins on a tall ridge that divides Lake Ann and Rainy Lake, crossing open slopes with tight switchbacks. You can see the trail zigging and zagging hundreds of feet below through wide-open gardens of heather and blueberries. Past the switchbacks, the trail ducks into the forest and continues quickly and directly for a couple more miles.

At 2.2 miles from Maple Pass and 7.0 miles from the beginning of the hike, turn left at a junction with the Rainy Lake Trail. This trail is paved and level. Sturdy wooden bridges cross several creeks, and educational plaques provide information about the surrounding old-growth forest. It's a civilized ending to a trail through such rugged terrain.

Larches frame Lake Ann on the Maple Pass Loop OLIVER LAZENBY

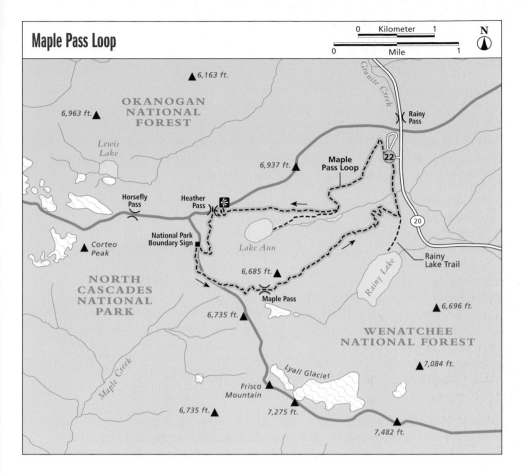

Miles and Directions

0.0 Start at the trailhead for the Lake Ann–Maple Pass loop trail. Take the trail to the right; you will return on the trail coming from the left.

1.3 At a junction with Lake Ann trail, go right toward Heather and Maple Passes.

2.3 Arrive at a viewpoint with views to Golden Horn, Whistler Mountain, and Cutthroat Peak.

4.1 Reach Heather Pass.

4.8 Arrive at Maple Pass.

7.0 Go left at the junction with the Rainy Lake Trail.

7.4 Arrive back at the trailhead.

23 | Tiffany Mountain

Sunshine, high–elevation, no crowds, beautiful scenery, and a short distance make Tiffany Mountain an exceptional outing. The open grasslands on the lonely east side of the Cascades offer easy travel to tall peaks, and this round dome is a fine example. The trail winds up the gentle side of the mountain, but from the summit you can look down at the steep ridges on the northwest side of the mountain. The ridges cradle little lakes and are covered in pines and western larches.

Distance: 4.4 miles out and back
Hiking time: About 2.5 hours
Difficulty: Moderate due to elevation gain
Trail surface: Dirt trail
Best season: June–Oct
Other trail users: Equestrians
Canine compatibility: Dogs must be leashed when in or around developed recreation sites, trailheads, interpretive trails, or campgrounds; voice control allowed in forest and wilderness areas. Always check at the trailhead for specific information regarding leash vs. voice control regulations.

Fees and permits: Northwest Forest Pass required to park at trailhead
Schedule: Open 24/7
Maps: USGS Tiffany Mountain; Green Trails No. 53: Tiffany Mountain
Trail contact: Okanogan National Forest, Methow Valley Ranger District; (509) 996-4000; www.fs.usda.gov/okawen
Special considerations: No water along the trail, so bring enough for you and your dog to last all day. This hike includes an elevation gain of 1,700 feet.

Finding the trailhead: From Winthrop go north on East Chewuch Road toward Pearrygin Lake State Park. In 6 miles, before crossing the Chewuch River, turn right onto FR 37. The pavement ends in 7.5 miles, and at 13 miles the gravel road comes to a junction with FR 39. Go left onto FR 39; in 3.2 miles park on the shoulder on the right (east) side of the road, just past a cattleguard. GPS: N48 39.77' / W119 57.97'

The Hike

Hikers come to Tiffany Mountain to bag a high peak, find some solitude, and enjoy the view. For the hiker who likes short, direct climbs to high peaks, Tiffany can't be beat. The only road in sight is the remote forest road you came in on, which winds into the distance between burned-out sticks. Even on weekends you won't run into many other hikers on this trail. Aside from FR 39, the mountains and wilderness are utterly uninterrupted as they stretch out before you and merge with the horizon.

The tall, round dome that is Tiffany Mountain reaches for the sun at 8,242 feet. From the summit, five broad ridges branch off and roll downhill into the creek valleys below. Western larches, whose needlelike leaves turn gold and fall off in autumn, cling to the north and west sides of every ridge. Glassy little lakes and ponds occupy the depressions between the ridges.

A colorful larch with Tiffany Mountain in the background OLIVER LAZENBY

The terrain, like most of the Okanogan Cascades, is gentle and rolling, but the ridges crumble into talus at their steepest sections. Many of the peaks in this area are taller than peaks at the crest of the Cascades. The open terrain lends itself perfectly to hiking and exploring. You won't find the thick vegetation that clings to the subalpine zones in the Cascades. Instead you will walk past wildflowers and golden grasses swaying in the high-elevation breeze.

The hike starts at Freezeout Pass at the Freezeout Ridge Trailhead, just north of a cattleguard. Park on the shoulder of the road, where there is room for about eight cars. That's usually enough space, as this hike is far from almost everywhere.

The trail follows Freezeout Ridge through trees burned in the 2006 Tripod Fire. The forest is regenerating and fireweed is crowding the burned slopes, providing color and vegetation to the otherwise barren landscape. Look closer and you can spot some young lodgepole pines reaching for light through the fireweed. The burned trees eventually give way to living spruce and lodgepole and whitebark pines that the flaming fingers of fire couldn't reach. All the while, the broad cone of

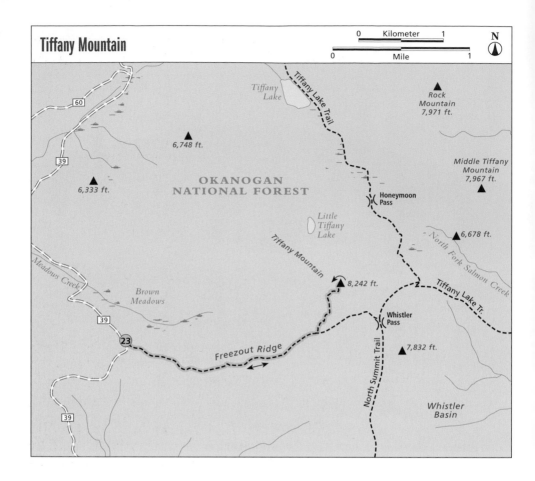

Tiffany Mountain is visible ahead of you. It looks distant and massive but is surprisingly close.

A sea of purple lupines mingle with the golden grasses on this peaceful ridge. Snowshoe hares and marmots pop in and out from jumbled boulders. From the trail you may see an assortment of birds, including golden eagles, mountain bluebirds, kestrels, and grouse.

A stripe of golden larches color the tree line on the north side of Freezeout Ridge in the fall. Wildflowers such as lupines, Indian paintbrush, and daisies bloom on the ridge in summer. Right before Freezeout Ridge broadens and begins climbing more steeply, you reach a junction and a signpost for Whistler Pass Trail. Take a left and continue directly up Tiffany Mountain. From here the trail is like a climber's trail. It's direct and braided in places but easy to follow.

Sweat up the open slopes toward the rocky summit. Tiffany Mountain is gentle and rounded on the southwest side, which the trail ascends. First-timers at Tiffany Mountain usually prepare for a disappointing view, as the ridge on the way up is so broad. But cliffs fall away on the northeast side of the mountain, making for a

Hiking along a trail fully loaded

spectacular view to the ridges and lakes below. The biggest lake beyond the loose east ridges is Tiffany Lake. Just beyond it, the Pasayten Wilderness stretches to the Canadian border. The mountains get increasingly more jagged to the west, and you can almost make out the sagebrush in the Okanogan Highlands to the east.

Don't forget to water your hound as you hunt for the "8,242" summit marker. The trip down is gravy, with epic views (but watch your step). Hikers with weary knees will appreciate hiking poles.

Miles and Directions

0.0   Start at the trailhead for Freezeout Ridge on FR 39.

0.8   After hiking through burned trees and brush, reach several stands of living trees.

1.5   Reach an open meadow above the initial forested ridge.

1.7   Go left at the signpost for Whistler Pass.

2.2   Reach the summit of Tiffany Mountain. Return the way you came.

4.4   Arrive back at the trailhead.

24 Manastash Ridge–Ray Westberg Trail

The Ray Westberg Trail—one of the best-loved hiking trails east of the Cascades—is a steep jaunt to a beautiful high point on Manastash Ridge. Many hikers use the trail to get in shape for longer trails and bigger mountains, but there's plenty to enjoy on the way up Manastash Ridge. The wildflowers are spectacular, as are the views of the Kittitas Valley and Stuart Range.

Distance: 4.2 miles out and back
Hiking time: About 2.5 hours
Difficulty: Moderate due to elevation gain
Trail surface: Dirt trail
Best season: Spring for wildflowers
Other trail users: Equestrians
Canine compatibility: Leashed dogs permitted
Fees and permits: No fees or permits required

Schedule: Year-round
Map: USGS Badger Gap
Trail contact: L. T. Murray Wildlife Recreation Area, Washington Department of Fish and Wildlife; (509) 925-6746; wdfw.wa.gov/lands/wildlife_areas/lt_murray/
Special considerations: This hike includes an elevation gain of 1,700 feet.

Finding the trailhead: From Seattle drive east on I-90 to exit 101 at Thorp. After exiting, turn right onto South Thorp Highway and follow it southeast for 2 miles. Turn right onto Cove Road and follow it south for 4.5 miles. Park on the gravel shoulder at the end of Cove Road. GPS: N46 58.06' / W120 38.73'

The Hike

In spring, Manastash Ridge can't be beat. The sky is usually clear, and the ridge is a convenient place to gain some elevation long before the snow melts in the Cascades. Several trails run from top to bottom, but the best and most popular route is the Ray Westberg Memorial Trail. The hike up Manastash Ridge is popular for its convenience—it's 5 miles from downtown Ellensburg and close enough for a day trip from Seattle on a sunny spring day—and it can be hiked almost year-round depending on the amount of snow. Locals hike the trail all year in snowshoes or boots equipped with traction devices.

Manastash Ridge is at least as beautiful as it is convenient. The ridge is covered in a variety of wildflowers, and as you climb you're treated to new species. Arrowleaf balsam root, phlox, desert buckwheat, and bitterroot are some of the most common flowers. The sagebrush and rabbitbrush could be considered old-growth—it towers overhead, perfuming the path. A variety of birds, including great horned owls and ospreys, can be seen overhead. Deer are common, and elk and bighorn sheep live nearby.

The ridge is the northernmost of a series of undulations that make up the desert moonscape between Ellensburg and Yakima. Northward movement of the West Coast is slowly buckling the ridges and pushing them ever higher. The climb is deceptive, because a series of knolls hides the top from view as you make your way up. You'll

Memorial Point on Manastash Ridge and Kittitas Valley below OLIVER LAZENBY

swear those tectonic plates are working extra hard and pushing the top of the ridge higher even as you climb.

From the trailhead at the end of Cove Road, walk past the gate and cross an irrigation canal. While the ditch may seem like an enticing spot for a doggie dunk pre- and post-hike, be aware that the water runs fast in the canal in spots, especially heading out from below the bridge. You can walk up or down the road to find slower runs, and it's a good idea to have your dog on a harness so that it's easy to pull her out of the water. You might even want to post a trail buddy downstream for added protection.

The trail begins climbing soon after and continues going almost straight up through sagebrush and ponderosa pines. After 1.0 mile of hiking, views of the Stuart Range begin, and they keep getting better the whole way up. Horned lizards scurry underfoot. There's a flat stretch after the first climb, but the trail soon continues climbing. Only a few trees provide shade on this trail, so start early if you're hiking on a hot, sunny day.

In 2.1 miles the trail arrives at Memorial Point, which has a rocky cairn and a multitude of memorials. One is for Ray Westberg, an Ellensburg High School wrestling coach and the trail's namesake.

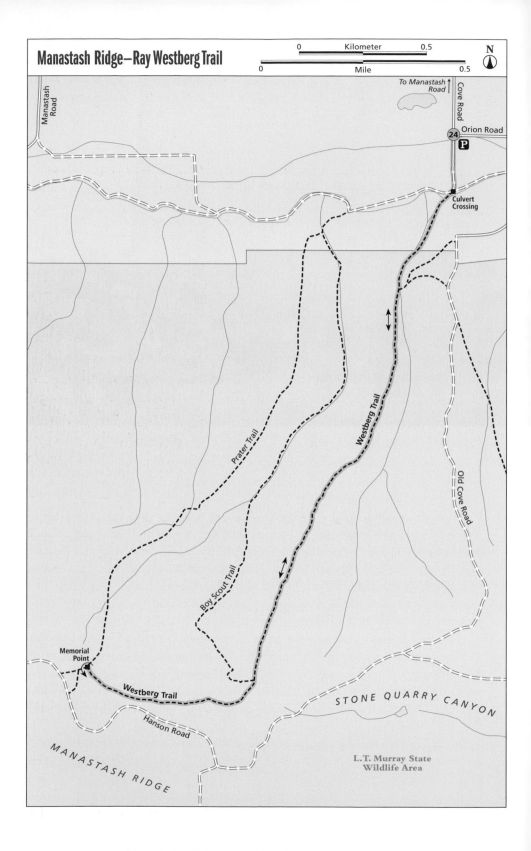

Manastash Ridge–Ray Westberg Trail

0	Kilometer	0.5
0	Mile	0.5

N

To Manastash Road

Manastash Road

Cove Road

24 Orion Road

P

Culvert Crossing

Prater Trail

Westberg Trail

Old Cove Road

Boy Scout Trail

Memorial Point

Westberg Trail

Hanson Road

STONE QUARRY CANYON

MANASTASH RIDGE

L.T. Murray State Wildlife Area

The view from the summit is spectacular. Mount Stuart reaches into the sky to the north. To the east, Manastash Ridge winds its way toward the Yakima River. Straight ahead you can see lush green irrigated fields of timothy hay, downtown Ellensburg, and the tall plateau of Table Mountain across Kittitas Valley.

Miles and Directions

0.0   Start from the parking lot near the end of Cove Road. Cross the gate and irrigation canal at the end of the road and bear left onto the trail to begin the hike.

1.5   Continue straight up the ridge, past a trail on the right.

2.1   Reach Memorial Point on top of the ridge. Return the way you came.

4.2   Arrive back at the trailhead.

THE LEGEND OF MEL'S HOLE

Mel's Hole, one of Washington's weirder legends, is a bottomless pit rumored to lurk somewhere on Manastash Ridge. The fabled hole with magical powers was made famous on the *Coast to Coast AM* radio show in 1997. Mel Waters, a caller on the radio show, claimed to have discovered a mysterious, rock-lined hole more than 15 miles deep. (He said he measured it with 20 pounds of fishing line and a weight.) Don't look too hard for the hole, because Waters claimed in 2008 that the hole is now elaborately camouflaged by the government. According to public records checks by local reporters at the time, no Mel Waters ever lived in Kittitas County.

25 Cowiche Canyon

One of the best rail trails in the state, Cowiche Canyon is an interesting pocket of wilderness surrounded by orchards, vineyards and other forms of civilization. Go in spring for the show of colorful wildflowers. Nearly anytime you go, a radiant blue sky will hang over the canyon's steep, rocky walls.

Distance: 6.2 miles out and back
Hiking time: About 3 hours
Difficulty: Easy due to flat terrain
Trail surface: Gravel
Best season: Spring for wildflowers; fall for colorful aspens
Other trail users: Bicyclists, equestrians
Canine compatibility: Leashed dogs permitted
Fees and permits: No fees or permits required

Schedule: Open 24/7
Maps: Cowiche Canyon maps, available online at Cowichecanyon.org; maps also sometimes available at a trailhead kiosk
Trail contact: Cowiche Canyon Conservatory, 302 N. Third St., Yakima 98901; (509) 248-5065; cowichecanyon.org
Special considerations: None

Finding the trailhead: East trailhead: From I-90, 2 miles east of Ellensburg, take exit 110 to merge onto I-82 South toward Yakima. Take exit 31A to merge onto US 12W. (If coming from downtown Yakima or points south on I-82, take exit 31 for US 12W.) In 3.8 miles turn left onto Ackley Road and then left again onto Powerhouse Road. Continue south on Powerhouse Road for 0.2 mile, and then turn right onto Cowiche Canyon Lane. In 1 mile, park at the widened end of the road. GPS: N46 37.33' / W120 36.90'

West trailhead: From US 12W, turn left onto Ackley Road, left again onto West Powerhouse Road, and then immediately right onto Naches Heights Road. In 3.8 miles continue left onto Zimmerman Road at an intersection with Dahl Road. Turn left onto Weikel Road 1.1 miles later, following signs for Cowiche Canyon. Park at the gravel lot at the end of the road.

Or from downtown Yakima, go west on Summitview Avenue for 9.1 miles. Turn right onto North Weikel Road and turn right in 0.5 mile at the signed trailhead. GPS: N46 37.88' / W120 39.93'

The Hike

In between acres of vineyards, rows of hops, and sprawling orchards, east of Yakima is a wild desert canyon. Cowiche Canyon is a convenient nook that's filled with sunshine, bare basalt rock, dark teal sagebrush, and dry-land flowers. Cowiche Creek meanders through this parched landscape, giving life to a flush of dense growth. Tiny fish mill in the channel. Just 10 feet away from this desert oasis, only the hardiest desert plants can suck moisture from the dry crust.

A trail leads through the canyon on an old railroad bed. Side trails leading up to the canyon rim intersect the straight path. One such path leads to a high plateau with views of Mounts Rainier and Adams and eventually to a winery and tasting room.

Many of the basalt canyons in Washington's desert are coulees carved by ice-age floods. Most of these canyons no longer have any water flowing through them.

Andesite formations in the canyon OLIVER LAZENBY

Cowiche is an exception. Cowiche Creek still flows through the walls of Columbia River basalt and Tieton andesite that it carved. Ice-age floods didn't reach this spot, but geologists still find plenty of interest in Cowiche Canyon. The Columbia River basalt flows that blanket the area and are visible in much of the canyon may be the single largest basalt flow in the world. Andesite from the world's longest andesite flow (which started in an ancient volcano near the Goat Rocks Wilderness) tops portions of the north wall.

In spring, wildflowers push through the crust of lichen and rocky soil toward the dark blue sky and puffy clouds. Clumps of desert phlox and bright yellow balsamroot flowers grow alongside the fragrant sagebrush. Bitterroot, whose flowers range in color from salmon pink to white, is especially abundant on the canyon's sloping walls. Only the plant's flower pushes its way above the ground. Below the surface, a carrot-like root stores energy for winter.

From the east end of the canyon, you'll pass several homes as the canyon walls slowly get steeper and narrower. Soon you'll see views of the creek. Cowiche Creek meanders back and forth through the canyon. Nine different bridges cross the creek on the rail trail. The junction to a winery and tasting room is marked with a sign at 1.2 miles. The trail toward the winery is worth exploring, even if not for the wine.

Cowiche Canyon

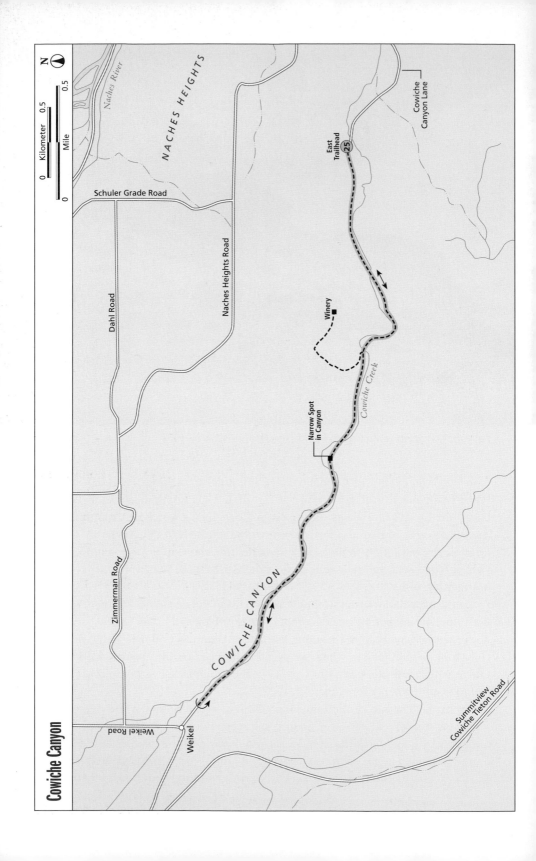

NACHES HEIGHTS

Naches River

Schuler Grade Road

Naches Heights Road

Dahl Road

Zimmerman Road

COWICHE CANYON

Weikel Road

Weikel

Narrow Spot in Canyon

Cowiche Creek

Winery

East Trailhead

25

Cowiche Canyon Lane

Summitview Cowiche Tieton Road

N

0   Kilometer   0.5

0   Mile   0.5

*Nootka Rose (*Rosa nutkana*) in Cowiche Canyon* OLIVER LAZENBY

You can gaze at the canyon from above and see the Cascade Mountains in the distance. The scenery is similar throughout the canyon, but subtle changes along the way keep the walk interesting.

Miles and Directions

0.0 Start from the east trailhead, at the end of Cowiche Canyon Lane.

1.2 Reach a junction with a trail up the north side of the canyon to the Wilridge Winery.

1.7 Pass through a narrow spot in the canyon.

3.1 Reach the west trailhead. Return the way you came.

6.2 Arrive back at the east trailhead.

26 Pack Forest

Discover peaks, lakes, and waterfalls hidden within a 50-mile network of trails.

Distance: 7.0-mile reverse lollipop
Hiking time: 4-5 hours
Difficulty: Moderate due to some elevation and sections of rugged trail
Trail surface: Dirt with some rugged sections
Best season: Hikable year-round; best Apr–Nov
Other trail users: Equestrian and bike use; hunting allowed; moderate foot traffic
Canine compatibility: Dogs must be under voice control. Always check at the trailhead for specific information regarding leash vs. voice control regulations.

Fees and permits: No fees or permits required
Schedule: Open 24/7
Maps: USGS Eatonville; trail map available online at www.packforest.org/education/11x17_low2.pdf
Trail contact: Pack Forest, 9010 453rd St. East, Eatonville 98328; (206) 685-4485; packforest.org
Special considerations: This hike includes an elevation gain of 1,300 feet.

Finding the trailhead: From Seattle take I-5 south to Tacoma, taking exit 127 for WA 512. In about 2 miles take the WA 7 exit toward Spanaway. Continue on WA 7 for roughly 22 miles to the signed entrance to the University of Washington Pack Forest on the left. Find visitor parking near the main office. GPS: N46 50.627' / W122 18.710'

The Hike

The Hugo Peak Trail begins at the gatehouse and heads somewhat steeply up the mountainside. At just over 1,700 feet, Hugo Peak is not exactly imposing, but the rough and narrow trail is a little overgrown in places, making the ascent a little challenging. The route cuts across a few trails and roads along the way, including the 1000 Road, a large loop open to vehicle traffic during the week. If you choose, you can cut out the lower section of the Hugo Peak Trail and just pick up the trail along the 1000 Road.

Near the top the trail suddenly changes into the 1081 Road, and you are soon at a somewhat confusing intersection. Head uphill to find the small, grassy clearing that is Hugo Peak. Over the years trees have grown to block out most of the view. Currently the view is limited to a narrow opening in the trees looking north toward the surrounding valleys. Take in the view, sign the summit register, and head back down to the intersection.

From Hugo Peak the next big destination is the waterfalls along the Little Mashel River, which are in the northern section of the park. To get there, just head

Old-growth Douglas fir on the Trail of the Giants
NATHAN AND JEREMY BARNES

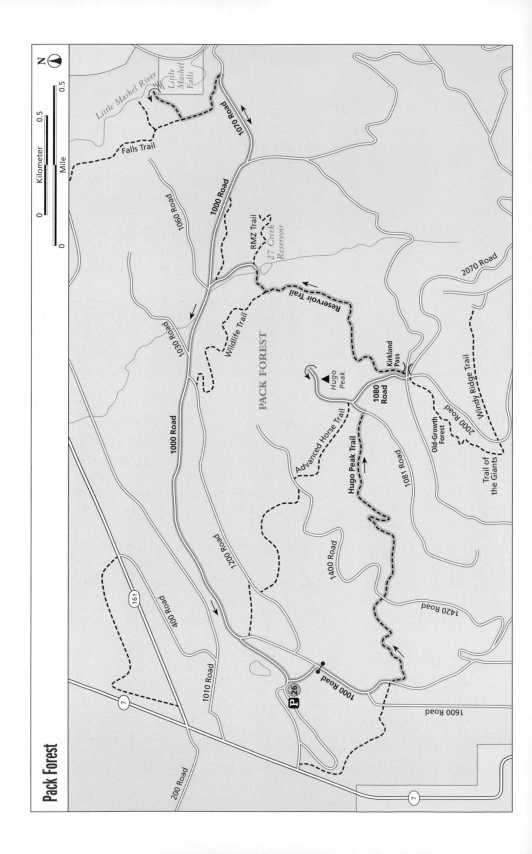

Pack Forest

N

0   Kilometer   0.5

0   Mile   0.5

Little Mashel River

Little Mashel Falls

Falls Trail

1070 Road

1060 Road

1000 Road

1030 Road

RMZ Trail

27 Creek Reservoir

Wildlife Trail

Reservoir Trail

PACK FOREST

Hugo Peak

Kirkland Pass

1080 Road

Advanced Horse Trail

Old-Growth Forest

2000 Road

Windy Ridge Trail

2070 Road

Trail of the Giants

Hugo Peak Trail

1081 Road

1400 Road

1420 Road

1000 Road

1600 Road

1200 Road

161

1000 Road

P 26

1010 Road

400 Road

200 Road

7

7

downhill on the 1080 Road toward Kirkland Pass, where most of the park's major roads meet. If you have some extra time, take a short stroll through the Trail of the Giants, a walk through a section of Pack Forest's old-growth woodland. From Kirkland Pass the more direct route is to follow the 1000 Road east to connect with the 1070 Road and eventually the Falls Trail. However, if you are looking for more trail time, you can take the Reservoir Trail that heads north and eventually leads to the 1000 Road.

Whichever way you go, you will soon be walking down the 1070 Road to the Falls Trail, which leads down into a canyon carved by the Little Mashel River. There are three waterfalls to see, starting with Tom Tom Falls (also known as Upper Little Mashel Falls), then Little Mashel Falls (often referred to as Bridal Veil Falls), and finally Lower Little Mashel Falls. The Falls Trail skips Tom Tom Falls, though you can catch glimpses of it by wandering a bit off-trail. The wide path quickly descends toward the river, with side trails branching off for views of the falls.

Follow the first branch for Little Mashel Falls, the largest of the three waterfalls. You'll have a choice between exploring the upper falls or the lower; we recommend starting with the upper, which takes you to the wide, flat rocks above the falls. This is the perfect place to settle down for lunch or a snack. If you prefer a closer look at Little Mashel Falls, take the steep trail down to the river. The trail can be very slippery, so use caution as you approach the falls. During summer, when the river flow is a little lighter, you can easily climb over the rocks and walk behind the falls. Again, the rocks are often slick, so be careful when clambering around beneath the waterfall.

To reach the final waterfall, Lower Little Mashel Falls, head back to the main Falls Trail and continue downward to the next branch. This trail is very overgrown, rough, and often muddy. Expect to be climbing over blowdowns and fallen logs. The trail ends in an overlook of the multitiered Lower Mashel Falls. It is easily worth the extra effort to see them. After you've had your fill, head back out to the 1000 Road and follow it back to the gatehouse.

Pack Forest is always open and almost always free of snow in winter. While some of the trails can be a little difficult to navigate, forest roads can take a hiker nearly anywhere in the park. With minimal elevation gain and easy access, this is a great pick for

HISTORICAL BACKGROUND

In the 1920s Charles Lathrop Pack was one of the richest men in the United States, with wealth built on timber and real estate. In 1926 he gave the University of Washington College of Forest Resources enough cash to purchase 334 acres of forestland, and the Charles L. Pack Experimental Forest was born. Today, Pack Forest has grown to a sprawling 4,300 acres, dedicated to forestry research, education, and recreation. With more than 50 miles of lowland trails, Pack Forest attracts hikers, mountain bikers, equestrians, and hunters year-round.

© ISTOCK.COM/DOLNIKOW

winter walks, hiking with youngsters, or bringing out the dog for an adventure. We suggest that you bring along a map, as the multiple roads and trails can be confusing, and maps are not always available from the gatehouse in winter. If you make it out to Pack Forest, we highly recommend taking the time to head out to the waterfalls—they are well worth the trip.

Miles and Directions

0.0 Start at the visitor parking near the main office and head right, up 1000 Road.

0.1 Walk past the gate on 1000 Road.

0.4 At the trail junction with the Hugo Peak Trail, turn left.

1.5 At the trail junction with 1081 Road, turn left.

1.6 Continue uphill past the Advanced Horse Trail toward the summit of Hugo Peak.

1.8 Reach the summit of 1,728-foot Hugo Peak. Retrace your steps to 1081 Road.

2.0 Turn to the left, following 1080 Road downhill.

2.1 At the trail junction with the Reservoir Trail, turn left.

2.8 At the trail junction with RMZ Trail, turn left.

3.1 Turn right onto 1000 Road.

3.5 Turn left down 1070 Road.

3.8 Turn left onto the trail leading down to the falls.

4.0 At the trail junction, head right to Mashel Falls. Head downhill to the lower falls.

4.2 Reach Mashel Falls. Turn around and head back to 1000 Road.

4.8 Turn right onto 1000 Road and follow it back to the parking area.

7.0 Arrive back at the trailhead.

27 Snowgrass Flat

The gardens beneath the Goat Rocks—which are the core of an ancient volcano— rival any other on Earth. This popular hike passes through miles of these magical gardens. Vibrant lupines and Indian paintbrush hug the sides of icy streams, and dark mountains with patchy snow hang overhead. Warning: There will be crowds. Make sure your dog is leashed and under close control.

Distance: 9.2 miles out and back
Hiking time: 5–7 hours
Difficulty: Difficult due to length and some elevation gain
Trail surface: Dirt trail
Best season: Aug–Oct
Other trail users: Equestrians and pack animals
Canine compatibility: Dogs must be leashed when in or around developed recreation sites, trailheads, interpretive trails, or campgrounds; voice control allowed in forest and wilderness areas. Always check at the trailhead for specific information regarding leash vs. voice control regulations.
Fees and permits: Northwest Forest Pass required to park at trailhead
Schedule: Open 24/7
Maps: Green Trails No. 302, Packwood; No. 303, White Pass; No. 304, Blue Lake; No. 335, Walupt Lake
Trail contact: Gifford Pinchot National Forest, Cowlitz Valley Ranger District; (360) 497-1100
Special considerations: Elevation gain of 1,200 feet to Snowgrass Flat

Finding the trailhead: From Morton drive 30 miles east on US 12 and turn right onto Johnson Creek Road (FR 21), 1.7 miles west of Packwood. In 15.5 miles turn left onto FR 2150, signed "Chambers Lake Campground." In 3 miles turn right onto FR 2150-040 and right again onto Spur 2150-405 (signed "Snowgrass Flat"). Continue to the trailhead and parking loop at the end of the road. GPS: N46 27.84' / W 121 31.17'

The Hike

A blanket of brilliant purple and red wildflowers cover the slopes and hang over the creeks underneath the Goat Rocks. The wildflowers are unbeatable, and aside from the volcanoes, the snowy mountains are the tallest and most rugged peaks between the Central Cascades and the Columbia River.

The flowery meadows can be seen in a day, and the nearby trails and peaks can fill multiple days of exploring. Strong hikers can make an optional 14.7-mile loop trip by returning on the Goat Ridge Trail and taking day hikes to Old Snowy Mountain and Hawkeye Point—one is a gentle but giant pile of loose rock with spectacular views; the other is a steep peak that makes a fine vantage for spotting mountain goats grazing around Goat Lake.

While the exploring is bountiful, so are the crowds. This makes day tripping to Snowgrass Flat a much simpler outing than having to hope and pray for a camping spot. Think twice about trying to camp at Snowgrass Flat on a weekend.

Wildflowers beneath the Goat Rocks OLIVER LAZENBY

The trail gets dusty in summer as hooved animals beat down on it. It's dustiest near the parking lot. At 1.8 miles cross Goat Creek on a sturdy bridge and enter the Goat Rocks Wilderness. The path climbs higher from here, and before you know it you're surrounded by wildflowers. As soon as the subalpine fir thins out, the dense lupines fill the high meadows. Lupines crowd one another, grasping for sunlight. They are most numerous and the star of the flower show. But between the dense clumps of lupines, you'll see bear grass, asters, Indian paintbrush, avalanche lilies, arnica, tiger lilies, Hooker's fairy bells, and much more.

The flowery climax is near Trail 96's junction with the Pacific Crest Trail (PCT). It's one of the state's best gardens, and it's in an idyllic setting. Snow melting from beneath the ridge of loose rock between Old Snowy Mountain and Ives Peak splashes between the clumps of flowers. Up above, hanging gardens of flowers drape themselves over rocky shelves of andesite. The rock here is all volcanic. The Goat Rocks are the withered ruins of an ancient volcano the size of Mount Adams.

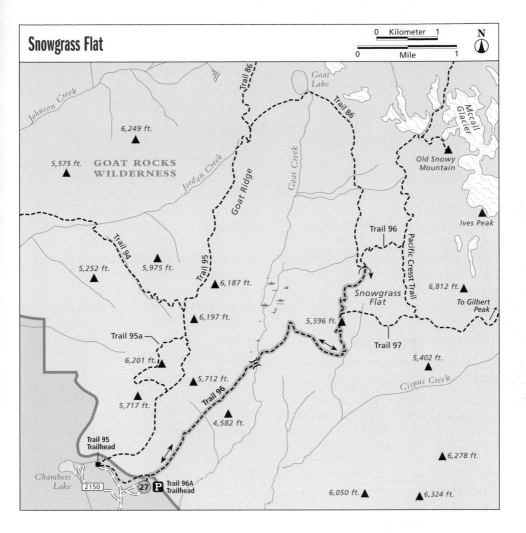

0   Kilometer   1

0   Mile   1

N

Goat Lake

Trail 86

Trail 86

Mccall Glacier

Johnson Creek

6,249 ft. ▲

Old Snowy Mountain ▲

Goat Creek

5,575 ft. ▲   **GOAT ROCKS WILDERNESS**

Jordan Creek

Goat Ridge

Ives Peak ▲

Trail 96

Pacific Crest Trail

Trail 94

5,252 ft. ▲   5,975 ft. ▲

Trail 95

▲6,187 ft.

Snowgrass Flat

6,812 ft.▲

To Gilbert Peak

▲6,197 ft.

5,596 ft. ▲

Trail 97

Trail 95a

5,402 ft. ▲

6,201 ft.▲

▲5,712 ft.

Trail 96

Cispus Creek

5,717 ft. ▲

▲ 4,582 ft.

Trail 95 Trailhead

▲6,278 ft.

Chambers Lake

2150   27 ℗   Trail 96A Trailhead

6,050 ft.▲   ▲6,324 ft.

Miles and Directions

0.0 Start at the trailhead for Trail 96A on Spur 2150-405.

0.2 Turn right onto Trail 96.

1.8 Cross Goat Creek on a wooden bridge and pass a campsite.

3.9 Reach the bypass trail, which bypasses the junction with the Lily Basin Trail and connects to the Pacific Crest Trail.

4.6 Arrive at Snowgrass Flat and the junction with the Lily Basin Trail, the end of this hike. You will want to spend some time exploring. *Option:* The Snowgrass Flat Trail continues from here to the PCT in 0.7 mile.

9.2 Arrive back at the trailhead.

28 Dog Mountain Loop

This steep day hike up Dog Mountain is worth the effort for the name alone, not to mention the swaths of wildflowers in season and the amazing views from the summit.

Distance: 6.8-mile loop
Hiking time: 3–6 hours
Difficulty: Difficult
Trail surface: Well-maintained dirt
Best season: Year-round or Mar–Dec, depending on frost line
Other trail users: Not suitable for mountain bikes
Canine compatibility: Leashed dogs permitted
Fees and permits: Northwest Forest Pass required
Schedule: Open 24/7
Maps: USGS Mount Defiance; Green Trails No. 430: Hood River; Trails Illustrated Columbia River Gorge

Trail contact: Gifford Pinchot National Forest, 10600 NE 51st Circle, Vancouver 98682; (360) 891-5000; www.fs.usda.gov/gifford pinchot
Special considerations: Traffic on this trail can be heavy, but the trail can absorb a lot of use without feeling crowded. The hike includes an elevation gain of 2,828 feet so you and your dog should be in shape and prepared. Bring enough water for the both of you to last all day because there is no water on the trail. Increasingly poison oak has become a problem along many parts of the Dog Mountain trail system, so beware, or wear long pants. Also keep your dog on a leash and away from poison oak.

Finding the trailhead: From Portland, take I-84 east to exit 44, Cascade Locks; cross the Columbia River and pay a toll on the Bridge of the Gods. Turn right, heading east on WA 14 for 12.5 miles to the well-marked Dog Mountain Trailhead on the left, at milepost 53. Restrooms are available 100 yards up from the old Dog Mountain Trailhead at the east end of the parking lot. The newer Augspurger Mountain Trailhead is just 50 feet west. GPS: N45 41.952' / W121 42.479'

The Hike

You like to hike with your dog, right? So you've got to hike up Dog Mountain, just because of the name alone. Surely your pooch will appreciate the eponymous name. Just make sure you bring plenty of water, because there aren't any streams along this hike. Bring warm layers too, as the top can be extremely windy.

The Dog Mountain trail system is heavily used by hikers, and the summit is often crowded on weekends; still, the mountain provides a peaceful and scenic hike. On a clear day, Mount Hood, Mount St. Helens, and Mount Adams are all visible from the top. Dog Mountain is also well known for wildflowers, especially during spring and early summer.

There are several different routes up the peak. The most scenic starts at the old trailhead at the east end of the parking lot. Take the "scenic" option on the first loop and return either the same way or via the more-gradual route down the back side—this description follows the latter route. You could reverse this by taking Augspurger Trail 4407 up, which takes 3.7 miles to get to the top and is not as steep. It makes a

Just 3.8 miles to the summit, Dog Mountain is a popular local hike. JIM YUSKAVITCH

better route down, because a steep climb followed by a more-gradual descent is easier on the knees.

From the east end of the parking lot, Dog Mountain Trail 147 climbs less than 0.1 mile to the public restrooms. Because of the trail's heavy use, it's better to use the facilities now than to have to go along the trail somewhere. The trail continues to climb steeply up dry, partially exposed switchbacks through fir and oak trees. The trail reaches the first junction at 0.5 mile. The right trail, to the east, is the more gradual and scenic option. The left trail, to the north, is the oldest route up Dog Mountain and has no views, lots of shade, and steep grades.

After taking the right trail, climb past a couple of good viewpoints of the Columbia River and across to Mount Defiance. At 2.0 miles the scenic and old trails rejoin. (A shorter option is to turn back at this point, descending on the opposite loop trail.) The main trail climbs in the shade for another 0.5 mile until it opens up to the Flowering Inferno. You might suppose this is a misprint or a bad pun on the *Towering Inferno*, but that's what the junction sign says. As the trail opens up into a meadow, the blooms of Indian paintbrush and balsamroot are spectacular. Even before these more noticeable flowers bloom, gold stars and buttercups add a yellow tint to the fresh green grass.

At 2.5 miles is a junction with a loop. This viewpoint junction is actually Puppy Dog Mountain, just a little bit smaller than the real thing. It used to be the site of a fire lookout, but this lookout—in use off and on since 1920—was dismantled in 1967. It is easy to see why from the view. The left route, to the northwest, is more scenic, especially if the balsamroot is in full bloom. It stays in the open, allowing a full view of the flowers, river, and the mountains beyond. The right trail to the east is a slightly longer option with fewer views.

After turning left, traverse the west face of Dog Mountain to the intersection with the summit trail. Continuing straight north is the Augspurger Trail; turning right, a little to the east, takes you to the top and the loop trail to the "Puppy Dog" junction. Turn right to reach the top. Just before the summit, the trail keeps going straight and passes a short spur trail on the left, to the north, through some low brush. This path is necessary to actually reach the highest point, but the view is better just below. The meadow below is a comfortable lunch and water spot.

From inside the grove of trees at the summit, you can see Mount Adams (and, through the branches, Mount St. Helens) to the north. Mount Hood and Mount Defiance are easily seen to the south across the river.

To return to the trailhead, there are three options: the way you came; the return trail to Puppy Dog junction; and the gentle, longer route back down the Augspurger Trail. For the last option, turn right down the 0.1-mile trail to the junction with the Augspurger Connector Trail. Turn right again, heading northwest, for the additional 3.7 miles back to the trailhead. The Augspurger Trail along the west face of Dog Mountain descends gradually, entering the trees after 0.5 mile. At 0.9 mile from the top, the trail intersects Augspurger Trail 4407.

Augspurger Trail 4407 continues north for 4.0 miles to the top of Augspurger Mountain. This side route offers occasional views through temperate forest. The forest service hopes to connect this ridge route with the Grassy Knoll Lookout Trail and access to the Pacific Crest Trail at Big Huckleberry Mountain. Turn left, heading south on Augspurger Trail 4407 for the trailhead, just 2.8 miles farther. The trail descends gradually along the side of Dog Mountain back toward the Gorge, down a couple of switchbacks and some dry, exposed scree slopes. Watch for poison oak.

Miles and Directions

- **0.0** Start from the Dog Mountain Trailhead off WA 14.
- **0.1** Pass the public restrooms.
- **0.5** At the junction of the scenic and old routes, turn right (east).
- **2.0** At the junction with the return of the scenic and old routes, stay right (north). *Option:* For a short hike, turn around and follow the old route back to the trailhead.
- **2.5** Reach the Flowering Inferno, Puppy Dog Mountain, and junction with loop trail; turn left (northwest). *Option:* Stay right (east) for a slightly longer climb to Dog Mountain.
- **2.8** At the junction with summit trail, turn right (east) to reach the top of Dog Mountain and the loop trail from Puppy Dog Mountain.

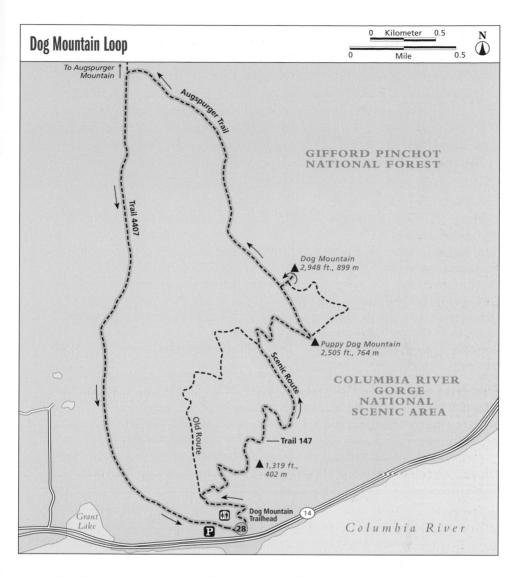

Dog Mountain Loop

To Augspurger Mountain

Augspurger Trail

Trail 4407

GIFFORD PINCHOT NATIONAL FOREST

Dog Mountain
2,948 ft., 899 m

▲ Puppy Dog Mountain
2,505 ft., 764 m

Scenic Route

Old Route

COLUMBIA RIVER GORGE NATIONAL SCENIC AREA

Trail 147

▲ 1,319 ft., 402 m

Grant Lake

Dog Mountain Trailhead

14

28

Columbia River

N

| 0 | Kilometer | 0.5 |
| 0 | Mile | 0.5 |

3.0 Bear right at the junction with the Augspurger Trail.

3.1 Reach the summit. *Option 1:* Turn around and follow the same route back to the trailhead.
Option 2: Follow the loop trail back to Puppy Dog Mountain, then follow either the scenic route or the old route back to the trailhead.

3.2 Return to Augspurger Trail; turn right (northwest).

4.0 At the junction with Augspurger Trail 4407, turn left (south).

6.8 Arrive back at the Dog Mountain Trailhead.

29 Lewis River

The Lewis River cascades down several grand falls on its way to the Columbia River. This section of trail features a high concentration of spectacular pools and waterfalls, as well as great views of the emerald water flowing through a deep valley of old-growth forest. The falls are not only large and plentiful but also close together, and the trail between them could hardly be easier.

Distance: 6.4 miles out and back
Hiking time: About 3 hours
Difficulty: Easy due to gentle terrain
Trail surface: Dirt trail
Best season: Apr–Nov
Other trail users: Mountain bikes, equestrians on first section of trail
Canine compatibility: Dogs must be leashed when in or around developed recreation sites, trailheads, interpretive trails, or campgrounds; voice control allowed in forest and wilderness areas. Always check at the trailhead for specific information regarding leash vs. voice control regulations.
Fees and permits: Northwest Forest Pass required to park at trailhead
Schedule: Open 24/7
Map: Green Trails No. 365: Lone Butte
Trail contact: Gifford Pinchot National Forest, 10600 NE 51st Circle, Vancouver 98682; (360) 891-5000; www.fs.usda.gov/gifford pinchot
Special considerations: None

Finding the trailhead: Leave I-5 in Woodland at exit 22. Turn left onto Lewis River Road (WA 503) and continue east for 23 miles to the town of Cougar. Continue straight through Cougar for 25 miles, past Lake Merwin, Yale Lake, and Swift Reservoir, to the Skamania County line, where the road becomes FR 90. Continue east for 13.7 miles and turn into the Lower Falls Recreation Area. Park near the restrooms and take one of several paths directly behind the restrooms toward the lower falls viewpoint. GPS: N 46 09.33' / W 121 52.88'

The Hike

Before the US Army Corps of Engineers installed dam after dam on the Columbia River, the lower falls on the Lewis River was a prime fishing spot for Native Americans. The 40-foot wall of whitewater presented an impassable barrier to salmon. What was once the end of the line for spawning salmon marks the beginning of an adventure to awe-inspiring waterfalls and lowland old-growth trees for hikers.

Upstream, the river is a raging torrent, flowing through the volcanic terrain below Mount Adams's Adams Glacier. Downstream, it's blocked by hydroelectric dams. In these woods, it flows gently and calmly, occasionally plunging over cliffs and cascading into deep pools.

The Lower Falls, a wide drop-off where the cool water splashes from platform to rocky platform, is just a couple hundred feet from the parking lot. To continue the hike from here, stay right along the river—following it upstream—through the tangle of trails to avoid getting lost in the maze of tents, RVs, barbecues, and kids on bicycles

Upper Falls on the Lewis River OLIVER LAZENBY

in the campground. For most of the hike you'll walk high above the river. On the trail you'll catch a glance of the shallow water only occasionally, but the tranquil sound of the stream is ever present. The trail winds through giant trees and beneath towering cliffs and caves colored in neon hues from lichen. Look for maidenhair ferns growing on the cliffs above the river. These delicate ferns with black stems like to grow on vertical cliffs near waterfalls. Here their roots find soil that drains quickly, but they can suck up constant moisture from the mist in the wake of the waterfalls.

The trail descends toward the river at each waterfall, where broad walls of whitewater roar off cliffs and into deep pools. The waterfalls are the main attraction, and the area around each falls seems to be made just for human enjoyment and relaxation, with warm rocks to rest on. Water flows, pools, and constricts in channels of solid rock before being released back into shallow stretches of river.

ANCIENT FORESTS

Trees grow quickly in southern Washington. Nearly all the ancient forests have been cut over and replaced with uniform second-growth stands. Around the Lewis River you'll find ancient trees and trees of varying height. The ground is littered with rotting logs, giving life to young hemlocks and cedars. The Lewis River was not named for Meriwether Lewis but for A. Lee Lewis, an early settler who homesteaded near the mouth of the river.

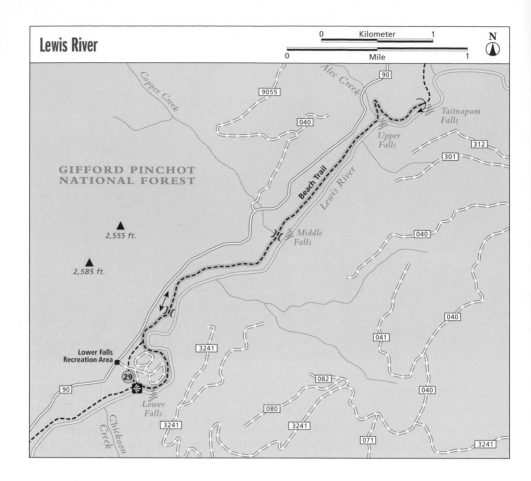

The second falls is a stout and turbulent set of rapids. The upper waterfall is perhaps the most scenic. It's about 60 feet tall, and the pool at the bottom is huge, making a wide opening in the forest canopy. To get the most waterfalls per mileage, continue another 0.7 mile to Taitnapum Falls, which you can see from the trail through an opening in the trees.

Miles and Directions

0.0   Start from the Lower Lewis River Falls Trailhead, just behind the restrooms at the Lower Falls Recreation Area. Begin hiking upstream, staying right along the river as you pass through the maze of trails in the campground.

0.2   Pass a boardwalk and stairs leading to a beach on the right.

1.6   Arrive at the middle waterfall.

2.5   Reach Upper Lewis River Falls. Past the falls, the trail climbs on a switchback.

3.2   Reach Taitnapum Falls, a good spot to turn around. Return the way you came.

6.4   Arrive back at the trailhead.

30 Ancient Lakes

This hike through a cliff-rimmed shrub-steppe desert ends at a waterfall tumbling into a spectacular set of lakes. Crumbling talus and 500-foot basalt cliffs covered in orange and green lichen surround the lush basin. The walk to the lakes is short, but there's plenty to explore in and above the basin.

Distance: 4.8 miles out and back
Hiking time: About 2 hours
Difficulty: Easy due to flat terrain
Trail surface: Dirt/sand road and trail
Best season: Mar–May
Other trail users: Equestrians, mountain bikers
Canine compatibility: Leashed dogs permitted
Fees and permits: Discover Pass required for parking

Schedule: Year-round
Map: USGS Babcock Ridge
Trail contact: Columbia Basin Wildlife Area, Washington Department of Fish and Wildlife, 6653 Road K NE, Moses Lake; (509) 925-6746; wdfw.wa.gov
Special considerations: None

Finding the trailhead: From Ellensburg drive east 40 miles on I-90 to exit 149 for WA 281. After exiting, turn left onto WA 281 North toward Quincy. After 5.6 miles turn left onto White Trail Road. In 7.8 miles turn left onto Ancient Lake Road (Road 9 NW). The road descends to Babcock Bench, a flat plateau above the Columbia River, and becomes gravel in 2.1 miles. From here continue 3.7 miles to the gravel parking lot for Ancient and Dusty Lakes. The trail starts at the gate at the south end of the parking lot. GPS: N47 09.58' / W119 58.84'

The Hike

The trail through Potholes Coulee showcases two of the most beautiful features of the Columbia Basin: rock deposited by one of the greatest basalt flows on the Earth's surface, and deep channels carved by floods during the last ice age. The coulee also hides something seldom found in the desert—lakes and waterfalls.

Between 15,000 and 13,000 years ago, Glacial Lake Missoula released some of the biggest floods on Earth. When the lake became full enough to lift the ice sheet that blocked its way to the west, water scoured eastern Washington. Potholes Coulee, like its neighbor to the north, Frenchmen Coulee, drained this floodwater toward the Columbia River. The water gouged a 500-foot-deep channel that is now home to a series of irrigation-fed lakes.

The abundant water is surrounded by parched rock and sagebrush. Thick vegetation clings to the edge of the lakes, and waterfowl including mallards and mergansers splash and feed. The glassy water of the three main lakes reflects the surrounding cliffs, buttes, and sky, which is usually blue in the Columbia Basin.

The Ancient Lakes Trail is beautiful from the very beginning, with views in every direction. The coulee is surrounded by orchards and vineyards, and you can see power

Hikers above Ancient Lakes OLIVER LAZENBY

lines from some parts of the hike. Most of the time, though, the deep walls cut off the surrounding civilization.

Start hiking on a sandy jeep trail at the south end of the parking lot. The trail is surrounded by rabbitbrush, big sagebrush, and wildflowers. Lupine, desert buckwheat, pink phlox, and arrowleaf balsamroot are the most prevalent flowers. The lavender-petaled sagebrush mariposa lily is also common along the north wall in the first 1.0 mile of the hike. Rattlesnakes sun their scaly bodies on rocks in the coulee, so keep your eyes on the trail.

From the jeep trail, the first trail to the left leads toward Ancient Lakes. It hugs the north rim of the coulee, where several waterfalls splash down the black cliffs, providing moisture for the bounty of vegetation. At 0.5 mile down the jeep trail is a second trail that also goes to Ancient Lakes, but it takes a path through the center of the coulee, away from the cliffs. The jeep trail continues south to Dusty Lake. The wall to the south of the trail isn't the south rim of Potholes Coulee but a 1,000-foot-wide finger that stretches directly down the center of the coulee. On the other side of the finger is Dusty Lake, a large lake that's popular for fishing.

The hike to the lakes and back is short, flat, and easy. But you can spend most of a day exploring around the coulee. From the lake basin, trails wander off in all directions. Trails wind around most of the lakes, and a trail with a short but steep talus scramble goes up the ridge south of the lakes. From there you can gaze 500 feet down into Dusty Lake and the south side of Potholes Coulee. A steep, scrambly trail leads past the waterfall to a network of paths that go to lakes and rock formations at the west end of the coulee.

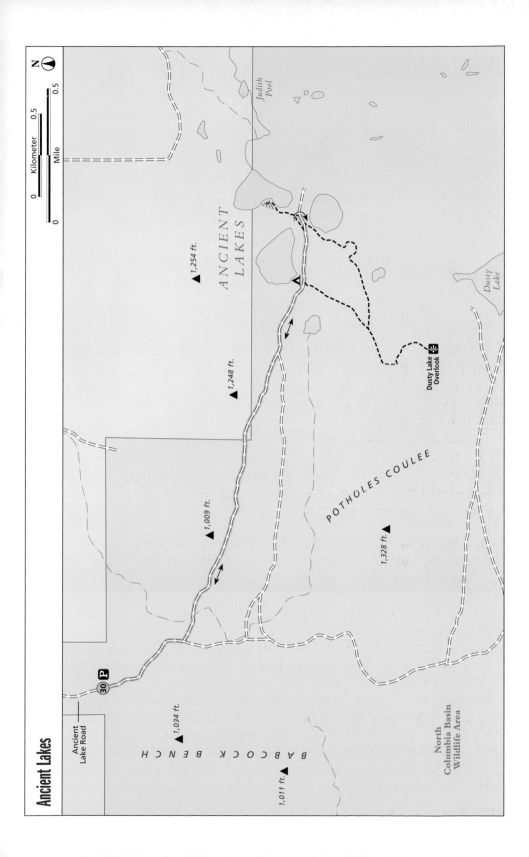

Ancient Lakes

Miles and Directions

0.0 Start at the Ancient and Dusty Lake Trailhead at the south end of the parking lot at the end of Ancient Lake Road (Road 9 NW).

0.5 Turn left off the jeep road and onto singletrack leading east into the coulee.

1.8 Arrive at a view of the waterfall on your left (north wall of the coulee).

2.1 Reach an established campsite at the westernmost lake.

2.4 Reach the end of the trail on a ridge between two lakes at the eastern edge of the coulee. Return the way you came.

4.8 Arrive back at the trailhead.

31 Northrup Canyon

The only natural forest in Grant County grows between the vertical walls of Northrup Canyon in Steamboat Rock State Park. The hike through the canyon is as rich in human history as it is in natural history. Remains of the Northrup family's homestead and other human artifacts are hidden in nooks between the 200-foot-tall walls. As the canyon narrows and begins to climb toward Northrup Lake, the trail is characterized by views of rugged granite and towering basalt.

Distance: 6.6 miles out and back
Hiking time: About 4 hours
Difficulty: Moderate due to steep sections
Trail surface: Gravel road through a flat valley, turning to dirt and rock trail over granite outcrops
Best season: Best Oct–June, when temperatures are cooler
Other trail users: Equestrians and mountain bikers

Canine compatibility: Leashed dogs permitted
Fees and permits: Discover Pass required
Schedule: Year-round, dawn until dusk
Map: USGS Steamboat Rock SE
Trail contact: Steamboat Rock State Park, PO Box 730, Electric City 99123; (509) 633-1304; stateparks.com/steamboat_rock.html
Special considerations: No overnight camping allowed

Finding the trailhead: From Coulee City drive north on WA 155 along Grand Coulee and Banks Lake for 22 miles to Northrup Road/Northrup Canyon Natural Area. Turn right onto the gravel road marked "Northrup Canyon Natural Area" and continue 0.7 mile to the parking lot. GPS: N47 51.94' / W119 04.98'

The Hike

Northrup Canyon has everything: Grant County's only forest, with lodgepole and ponderosa pines, fir, and quaking aspen; meadows, cliffs, chunks of bedrock granite protruding in areas where ice-age floods scoured away the much more recent basalt; an old homestead with vacant buildings succumbing to gravity; and a trout-filled lake.

The lush valley, bare rock, and sharp granite ridges between the towering walls of Northrup Canyon once bustled with human activity. Four generations of the Northrup family lived between the canyon walls, where they grew fruit and vegetables and raised animals. People from neighboring counties rode into the canyon on horses and wagons on an old stagecoach road on the south wall of the canyon to sample the Northrups' produce.

Despite the many human artifacts hidden in its forgotten corners, Northrup Canyon is now a nature sanctuary and a great place to get away from the humans at nearby Banks Lake. Cougars and bears spend time in the canyon, and it's a winter home for as many as one hundred bald eagles. In fact, the stagecoach road near the beginning of the trail is closed in winter to protect roosting eagles.

As the trail enters the canyon near Banks Lake, the desert fades away and becomes

Basalt cliffs in Northrup Canyon OLIVER LAZENBY

a forest (or at least what passes for a forest in Grant County). Big pines and firs cast shade over the old dirt road in the first section of the hike. Later on, a creekbed provides moisture for quaking aspens, serviceberry, and squaw currant.

The trail to the right about 200 yards from the trailhead is an old stagecoach road that used to be the main road between Almira and Brewster. It leads to a plateau atop the south wall of the canyon, with views back toward Steamboat Rock. Stay left and continue on the road. This can be confusing, because the Northrup Canyon Trail is a road and the old stagecoach road is a trail.

On the left side of the trail in the first 0.25 mile of the hike is one of several large can dumps. The piles of rusted cans were left behind by Grand Coulee Dam construction workers. Apparently garbage becomes artifact at some point, because the cans are considered a historical site and should not be moved.

After the initial forested sections, you'll pass through an open meadow with views of the canyon walls. On your left, several giant ovular chunks of basalt seem to be leaning against one another on the canyon wall. Views of basalt formations surround you in all directions. Stinging nettle and even some poison oak line portions of the road in the meadow, but the road is plenty wide, and these noxious plants are easy to avoid.

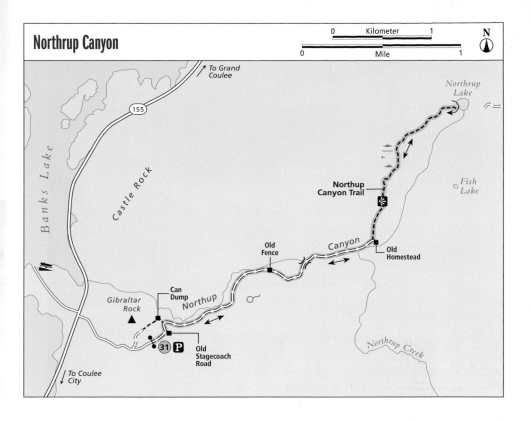

Kilometer

0   1

Mile

0   1

N

To Grand Coulee

Northrup Lake

155

Banks Lake

Castle Rock

Northup Canyon Trail

Fish Lake

Old Fence

Canyon

Old Homestead

Can Dump

Gibraltar Rock

Northup

Northrup Creek

31 P

Old Stagecoach Road

To Coulee City

The views continue along the pleasant road until you reach the remains of the homestead. Several long-abandoned buildings are succumbing to the pull of gravity, while white and lavender lilacs and a peach tree live on nearby. The newer white building was used seasonally by park rangers until recently. Bearing right along the south wall of the canyon will lead you to even more forgotten fruit trees.

The hike to the homestead is gentle, scenic, and easy. Turning around here makes for a good short hike, but the gem of this hike is the next 1.4 miles of trail that climbs up the canyon toward Northrup Lake.

From the homestead the trail climbs steeply from the valley floor. Look for a sign with a hiker on it near an old henhouse. The trail goes north from the homestead. In this section, a bare spine of granite bedrock runs down the center of the canyon. Granite is rare in the Columbia Basin. Actually, any rock other than basalt is rare here. The granite ridge was covered by basalt until ice-age floods eroded the basalt from the canyon floor, exposing the ancient granite. The granite gives this steep, hilly section of the hike a high alpine feel. If you forget where you are, you may expect to see mountain goats. All the while, basalt cliffs still loom high on either side of the ridge.

After a steep climb, the trail levels out and you pass through a maze of granite and crumbling basalt boulders shaded by pine trees. This upper section of trail is also packed with wildflowers, including alumroot, balsamroot, lupines, and bluebells.

Australian Cattle Dog resting on a piece of driftwood

The spring-fed Northrup Lake is small, full of trout, and a haven for birds. Cliff swallows, western kingbirds, tanagers, meadowlarks, and hummingbirds play near the blue water, and you may see falcons, ravens, hawks, eagles, or turkey vultures flying high above.

The canyon has several other sights to explore that are not on the trail. You can discover several seasonal lakes, or more can dumps and other human artifacts. The bare granite face of Gibraltar Rock, near the equestrian parking lot, is a hot spot for rock climbers.

If you make it back to your car and you're hungry for more, head for Steamboat Rock, which is a couple miles west. The hike up Steamboat Rock is a short, steep grind up to a plateau with 360-degree views of Grand Coulee and 600 acres of sagebrush-filled wandering.

Miles and Directions

0.0 Start at the trailhead at the end of Northrup Road / Northrup Canyon Natural Area.

0.1 Bear left to stay on the trail. The old stagecoach road takes off to the right.

0.2 Pass a portion of a historical can dump on the left side of the trail.

1.5 Cross Northrup Creek on a wooden bridge.

1.9 Arrive at the site of old homestead with several buildings. The trail continues to the north behind the henhouse. Look for a sign with a hiker near the buildings.

2.2 Climb a granite ridge to a view back down into the canyon and toward the homestead.

3.3 Reach Northrup Lake. Return the way you came.

6.6 Arrive back at the trailhead.

© ISTOCK.COM/BETYARLACA

LIFE IN NORTHRUP CANYON

John Warden Northrup arrived in the canyon that now bears his name in 1829 after several failed marriages, career changes, and years of wandering in the Northwest. The fertile soil, steady supply of water, and good fishing attracted Northrup. When he moved to the canyon, it was the wettest, most fertile spot in the county, as Grand Coulee Dam and its reservoirs did not yet exist.

Northrup quickly got to work creating an irrigation system from the spring-fed stream and planting the first orchard in Grant County. He grew twenty-nine varieties of trees, along with vegetables, grains, and animals. He also successfully raised cotton, tobacco, peanuts, and a family in the canyon. By the time the last Northrup moved away from the canyon in the late 1920s, four generations had lived between the basalt walls.

The Northrups weren't just subsistence farmers. The road up the south side of the canyon was the main route between Brewster and Almira, and people came from all over Grand, Lincoln, and Douglas Counties to buy fruit and vegetables from the Northrups' farm. By the turn of the twentieth century, food from the canyon was even going to the fancier restaurants of Spokane.

The Northrups owned the majority of the canyon, but several other families also called the canyon home. The Schiebner brothers, who were hired by the government to build the section of stagecoach road through the canyon, owned a sawmill 1 mile from the entrance to the canyon. The Dillman family, who farmed goats, lived at the canyon entrance.

According to Norman Northrup, John Warden Northrup's great-grandson, the canyon was also home to a cougar with a weird sense of humor (she seemed to enjoy scaring visitors), and it was the scene of a murder.

When John Warden Northrup's health began to fail in 1894, his third wife, Caty, leased part of the farm to Israel Sanford. Shortly after, in a dispute over the ownership of fruit trees, Israel killed Caty in the sagging log house just south of the white house just before the present-day trail starts climbing toward Northrup Lake. Sanford was later acquitted by a jury for being of unsound mental health.

When John Warden Northrup died in 1901, his son George took over the farm with his wife, Joella. George had worked as a sheriff, banker, real estate agent, journalist, lawyer, preacher, and miner, and he never liked farming. When he split up with Joella over financial problems a few years later, Joella took over the farm.

Joella, with the help of a hired man and her children, worked hard to make the farm pay. She clawed her way out of the debt that George had accumulated and later became known as the "Canyon Lady." In his book *Northrup Canyon: A Living History*, Norman Northrup describes Joella as "a tough, no nonsense, feisty lady, who was not afraid to spit in the eye of the devil himself."

During the next twenty-five years, the canyon became known as a great place to picnic or visit when passing through on the stagecoach road. The road got a lot of traffic at the beginning of the twentieth century. It not only connected Almira and Brewster but also military forts in Spokane, Chelan, and Okanogan. According to Norman Northrup's book, when the Northrups spotted people coming through the canyon, they always put another chicken in the pot.

In 1926 or 1927, depending on the source, Joella and her son Charlie—the last Northrups on the farm—packed up and left. Water had become scarce in the canyon. Also, the rise of trucking had made their produce less profitable.

To learn more, check out *Northrup Canyon: A Living History*. The first half of the forty-eight-page self-published book is a historical account of the canyon; the second half is full of wild stories and tall tales about a tornado dropping thousands of fish into the canyon, the cougar with a weird sense of humor, and the Northrup boys killing snakes from horseback with whips.

32 Kamiak Butte Pine Ridge Trail

The Pine Ridge Trail makes a quick loop up and down one of the Palouse region's rare mountains. The 2.5-mile trip starts in a dense forest, where the trail begins to switchback up a steep hillside to the top of a ridge. From the ridge, the wrinkles and folds and patches of wheat and lentils of the Palouse stretch in all directions. Photographers flock to the Palouse to capture its wide-open beauty, and Kamiak Butte is a unique vantage point.

Distance: 2.5-mile loop
Hiking time: About 1.5 hours
Difficulty: Easy due to short distance and a smooth trail
Trail surface: Dirt and gravel trail
Best season: Spring through early summer
Other trail users: Equestrians
Canine compatibility: Leashed dogs permitted

Fees and permits: Discover Pass required for parking
Schedule: Year-round
Map: USGS Albion
Trail contact: Kamiak Butte County Park; (509) 397-6238
Special considerations: None

Finding the trailhead: From Pullman drive north on WA 27 for 12 miles. Turn left onto Clear Creek Road and continue onto Fugate Road, following signs for Kamiak Butte County Park. In 1 mile turn left into Kamiak Butte County Park; follow the road all the way to the wooded park and day-use parking lot. GPS: N46 52.22' / W117 09.15'

The Hike

The rolling hills that make up the Palouse region of southeastern Washington are surprisingly uniform. From above, your eyes can trace lines and ridges for miles; there is no shortage of beauty, but the ripples are all a similar size. The landscape is a giant version of a sandy beach covered in emerald-green grasses and crops. That's because it was formed by huge flows of water released by Glacial Lake Missoula ice-age floods. North of Pullman, two islands of quartzite protrude from the gentle landscape—Steptoe Butte and the slightly taller Kamiak Butte. From Kamiak Butte, the fertile Palouse farmland looks like a wrinkled green quilt with patches of every shade. At 3,641 feet, Kamiak Butte may not be tall compared to the mountains of the Cascades, but it towers over its surroundings.

Kamiak Butte is an incredible example of microclimates. The north and south sides of the butte have very different vegetation. The butte's north face is covered in pines, firs, western larches, thick vegetation, and even some cedars. The trail is mostly on this side of the butte, and it winds through a shaded understory of thimbleberries, lady ferns, miner's lettuce, Nootka rose, Oregon grape, and mallow ninebark bushes with their thick bouquets of little white flowers. The sunnier south slope is a different world. Because the sun bakes it all day, it's mostly free of trees and the lush vegetation of the north slope. Instead it supports the kind of dry grassland ecosystem that covered the Palouse before agriculture took over.

The Palouse region from Kamiak Butte OLIVER LAZENBY

The butte has even more to show off than views of two entirely different eco-systems. From the high point of the butte and most of the ridge along the top, you can see Pullman and Moscow to the south. On clear days, the Blue Mountains are also visible. The sea of solidified magma and silt continues rolling to the north. The region's other quartzite island, Steptoe Butte, is 15 miles northwest of Kamiak Butte and just 29 feet lower in elevation. The rolling hills, waving sea of grains, and rustic barns of the Palouse are popular with photographers, and Kamiak Butte offers a rare chance to get high above this uniform landscape.

The butte is really a long ridge. The Pine Ridge Trail switchbacks up to the low point on the ridge and then follows the ridge dividing the two microclimates. At a high point at the west end of the ridge, the trail dives back into the forest. A short spur from the ridge atop the butte leads to a viewpoint before dead-ending at private property. From the high point, the views are about the same as they are along the ridge.

On top of the ridge, the sunbaked soil is too dry for firs or larches. The occasional deep-rooted ponderosa pine manages to carve out an existence here, but mostly the ridge is covered in wildflowers that bloom from March to July. Indian paintbrush, shooting stars, and asters add bright highlights to the rolling green backdrop. The flowers on top of the butte are stunning, but the flowers in the forest are even more impressive because they are so rare in eastern Washington. Among the shade-loving

Foxglove (Digitalis *spp.*) *on Kamiak Butte's shadier north slope* OLIVER LAZENBY

species more typical of the Cascades are trillium, foxglove, glacier lilies, and several orchids, as well as flowering dogwoods and hawthorns.

The wildflower season is long on Kamiak Butte thanks to their diversity. The best time to hike the butte is the peak of the flower season in April. Early summer is also a great time to hike Kamiak Butte, because the rolling fields of wheat show their dark green hues from the middle of June until late July, when the harvest begins.

The loop can be hiked either way, but if you go left (clockwise), you reach the ridge faster. Start up the trail from the lower parking lot and continue going straight when you encounter a trail to the right in 200 feet. When you descend from the high point of the ridge, the vegetation quickly changes. Soon you are in a dense, humid forest choked with small trees and shrubs. The dense vegetation provides food and cover for deer, voles, porcupines, wrens, sparrows, warblers, and the rufous-sided towhee. A young bull moose and its grumpy mother made Kamiak Butte County Park their home in winter 2012.

A section of this trail passes through an old ski run that the park service built in the 1950s. It soon failed because of a lack of snow. Nearby trees quickly reseeded the open slope, making for a thick growth. Northern saw-whet, pygmy, and great horned

WHAT IS A STEPTOE?

Kamiak Butte, named for Yakama Indian Chief Kamiakin, is a classic steptoe—an isolated mountain of bedrock that was surrounded by a lava flow. The result is a relatively flat or uniform landscape with a surprisingly tall mountain poking out of it. Several times in its life, Kamiak Butte has been an island surrounded by fiery magma.

The magma has cooled, but the steptoes in the Palouse remain ecological islands with different flora than the surrounding grasslands. Dense trees cover most of the butte, which is home to a variety of animals and wildflowers rarely seen in eastern Washington.

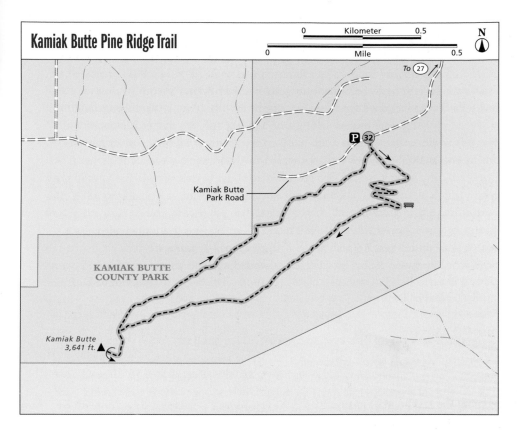

Kamiak Butte Pine Ridge Trail

0 — Kilometer — 0.5

0 — Mile — 0.5

N

To (27)

P (32)

Kamiak Butte
Park Road

KAMIAK BUTTE
COUNTY PARK

Kamiak Butte
3,641 ft. ▲

owls hang out in the tops of the pines. At the base of the butte is a quiet campground with shaded car and walk-in campsites and a picnic area with restrooms and a playground. The 298-acre park used to be a state park, but Whitman County took it over in 1976 when the state threatened to close it. You'd be hard pressed to find a more pleasant outing in a county park.

Miles and Directions

0.0 Start from the trailhead at the lower lot in the county park's day-use area.

0.1 Go left at the fork for the more direct route up the ridge.

0.3 Begin switchbacks; you'll shortly pass a bench.

0.5 Bear right at the top of the switchbacks, following a sign for the Pine Ridge Trail. Go right again to continue up the ridge.

1.5 Reach an intersection. Go left for the 0.1-mile spur to the summit, or turn right to complete the loop without the spur.

2.4 Arrive back at the first intersection and go left toward the parking lot.

2.5 Arrive back at the parking lot.

33 Bowl and Pitcher Loop

Hike through rock gardens, draws, and uplands of Riverside State Park, Washington's second largest. The park covers 10,000 acres of forests, rocky canyons, and riverfront, as well as several miles of the splashing and frothing Spokane River. A large section of this hike follows the 25-Mile Trail, which is a 25-mile-long loop through Riverside State Park. Signposts mark much of the 25-Mile Trail.

Distance: 5.5-mile double loop
Hiking time: About 3 hours
Difficulty: Easy to moderate
Trail surface: Dirt trail
Best season: Spring through fall; winter if there isn't snow cover
Other trail users: Bicyclists and equestrians
Canine compatibility: Leashed dogs permitted
Fees and permits: Discover Pass required
Schedule: Open 24/7
Maps: Riverside State Park Multiuse Trail Map, produced by the Inland Empire Backcountry Horsemen, PO Box 30891, Spokane 99223;

www.iebch.com (map may be purchased at the state park). National Geographic Washington topo on CD-ROM, disk 4, and Montana Mapping & GPS LLC's hunting and GPS maps are good topos of the area.
Trail contact: Riverside State Park, 9711 Charles Rd., Nine Mile Falls 99026; (509) 465-5064; riversidestatepark.org
Special considerations: This is a fairly complicated route to follow, so be sure to keep your map handy and follow your progress. On the last 3.4 miles of this hike (and some sections before that), follow the 25-Mile Trail markers.

Finding the trailhead: From exit 281 on I-90, take Division Street north to Francis, which is WA 291. Turn west (left) onto WA 291 and go 3.8 miles to the junction with Rifle Club Road. A sign here points to the Bowl and Pitcher area. Turn left on Rifle Club Road and drive 0.4 mile southwest to Aubrey L. White Parkway. Turn left on Aubrey L. White Parkway and drive 2 miles south to the Bowl and Pitcher area, which includes a campground and day-use area. The trailhead is on the west side of the area, at the east end of the Swinging Bridge. Signs point out the way. There is plenty of parking, restrooms, and a campground close to the trailhead. The Riverside State Park Multiuse Trail Map may be helpful here. GPS: N47 41.801' / W117 29.818'

The Hike

Before you cross the Swinging Bridge and begin your hike, read the reader board at the east end of the bridge. The Bowl and Pitcher rock formation is to your right as you cross the Swinging Bridge. Once across the bridge the course climbs a short distance to the junction with the 25-Mile Trail. Turn right (north) at the junction onto the 25-Mile Trail.

As you hike north the route works its way through the dark rock outcroppings. You will reach the junction with Trails 210 and 211 in 0.3 mile. Turn right at the junction, staying on the 25-Mile Trail, and start the first loop. You soon reach another junction, where you'll hike straight ahead, staying on the main trail. To the right

Bowl and Pitcher FRED BARSTAD

below the trail, the Spokane River froths and sloshes through a set of rapids. The track follows the top of the riverbank as you hike northeast, well above the clear, rushing waters.

At 0.6 mile from the trailhead, the course goes under some power lines. There is an unsigned trail junction 0.25 mile farther along. The trail to the left is a shortcut, but it misses some of the best river views on this hike. Bear right here, staying on the main trail, which follows the riverbank. A column of rock called the Devils Toe Nail rises from the center of the frothing river, 0.3 mile farther along. Soon the track passes mile marker 20. There is another trail junction just past the mile marker. Turn left here, temporarily leaving the 25-Mile Trail. The route climbs a short distance west to a junction with Trail 211, which is an abandoned roadbed. The trail that turned left off the 25-Mile Trail 0.5 mile back also rejoins the route (coming in from the southeast; see map for clarification) here.

Turn left on Trail 211 and hike south. Three-tenths of a mile after leaving the junction, rock outcroppings rise above the trail on your right. The course returns to the junction with Trail 210 and the 25-Mile Trail in another 0.2 mile. This junction, 1.6 miles into this hike, is the end of the first loop and the beginning of the second. If you would like to make this a shorter outing, you can retrace your steps from here back to the Swinging Bridge Trailhead.

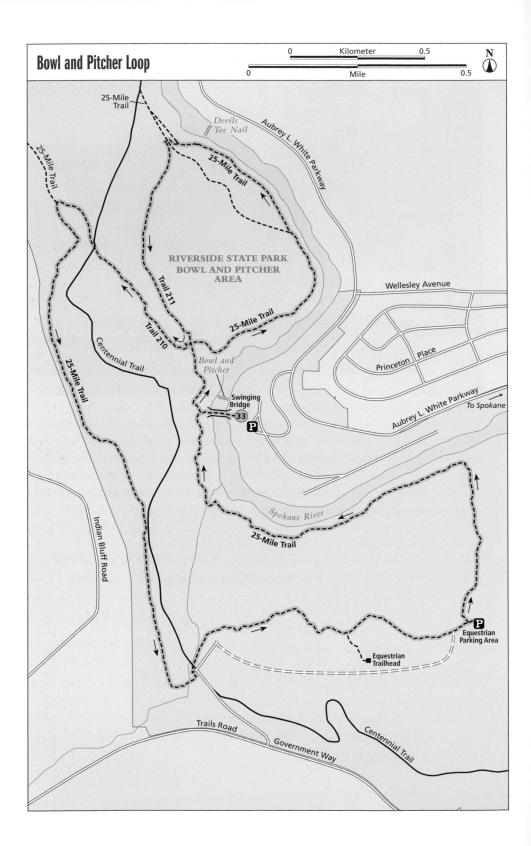

Kilometer

0   0.5

Mile

0   0.5

N

25-Mile Trail

Devils Toe Nail

Aubrey L. White Parkway

25-Mile Trail

25-Mile Trail

RIVERSIDE STATE PARK
BOWL AND PITCHER
AREA

Wellesley Avenue

Trail 211

Trail 210

25-Mile Trail

Centennial Trail

25-Mile Trail

Princeton Place

Bowl and Pitcher

Swinging Bridge

33

P

Aubrey L. White Parkway

To Spokane

Spokane River

25-Mile Trail

Indian Bluff Road

Equestrian Trailhead

P

Equestrian Parking Area

Trails Road

Government Way

Centennial Trail

To continue on to the second loop, turn right at the junction and head west on Trail 210. The track makes a couple of switchbacks then continues to climb to the northwest, passing a viewpoint. In 0.4 mile Trail 210 crosses the wide, paved Centennial Trail. In a little more than 0.1 mile more, you reach the junction with Trail 200, which is marked on a trail sign. Turn left here and quickly reach the junction with the 25-Mile Trail, which you will be following all the way from here back to the Swinging Bridge Trailhead. By the time you reach this junction, you have climbed a little more than 200 feet of elevation from the junction with Trail 211 where you started this loop.

Turn to the left on the 25-Mile Trail and head south. In the open areas, lupine and death camas sprout beside the trail. After climbing another 150 feet in 0.3 mile, the track levels out. The course follows an abandoned grade for 0.3 mile then turns left, leaving the grade and making a couple of descending switchbacks. The route then flattens out on a meadow-covered bench beneath some power lines. This section of the route parallels the Centennial Trail, which is to your left (east). After following the power lines for about 0.6 mile, the tread turns left and descends to another junction with the Centennial Trail. At this point you have hiked 3.6 miles since leaving the Swinging Bridge Trailhead.

Turn left at the junction onto the Centennial Trail. Walk a few yards to the north, passing the junction with the road that leads to the equestrian trailhead. Then turn right, staying on the 25-Mile Trail and leaving the paved Centennial Trail. The route now heads east-northeast and shortly reaches a trail junction where you bear right and quickly cross an abandoned roadbed. In 0.3 mile the trail turns right on another abandoned roadbed and descends a short distance to the junction with Trail 101. Bear right here, then turn quickly left on another abandoned roadbed. There are "pipeline" signposts at these turns. Shortly, you turn right, leaving the pipeline. A little farther along is another junction. The trail (roadbed) to the right leads 100 yards to an equestrian trailhead. Hike left (east) here, staying on the 25-Mile Trail.

In 0.1 mile the route turns right, leaving the roadbed, and soon crosses two abandoned roadbeds. Then you enter the parking area for another equestrian trailhead. Turn left (northeast) at the parking area on a road and soon bear left, staying on the main road (25-Mile Trail). You quickly pass two more junctions—bear left at both. Then the route crosses the pipeline road and Trail 101. You will reach the junction with Trail 100 0.2 mile past the second equestrian trailhead.

At the junction with Trail 100, the 25-Mile Trail turns to the left (west), with the Spokane River below to your right. The track follows the river west for about 0.6 mile. In places, other trails parallel the main trail. There are several junctions with these side trails. After 0.6 mile the course turns right to head north for the remaining 0.3 mile to the junction next to the Swinging Bridge. Turn right here and cross the bridge to the trailhead. *Note:* The two loops described here can easily be hiked separately from the same trailhead.

Miles and Directions

0.0 Start at the Swinging Bridge Trailhead and cross the Swinging Bridge.

0.4 Turn right onto the 25-Mile Trail, starting the first loop.

1.1 Turn left on Trail 211 (roadbed).

1.6 Turn right at the junction with Trail 210 and the 25-Mile Trail.

2.0 Cross the Centennial Trail.

2.1 Turn left on the 25-Mile Trail.

3.6 Cross the Centennial Trail again.

4.0 Pass a roadbed to an equestrian trailhead.

4.3 Pass another equestrian trailhead.

4.5 At the junction with Trail 100, stay on the 25-Mile-Trail.

5.5 Arrive back at the Swinging Bridge Trailhead.

MUSKRAT

The muskrat (*Ondatra zibethicus*) is not a close relative of the beaver, despite their many similar habits. Muskrats are 16 to 25 inches in length (including the nearly hairless tail) and may weigh up to 3 pounds. They are covered with thick, glossy, brown fur that has been and is still to some extent valuable. Excellent swimmers, muskrats never stray far from water. Like beavers, they can stay underwater for 15 minutes or slightly longer.

© ISTOCK.COM/GRIGORII_PISOTCKII

34 Liberty Creek-Camp Hughes Loop

Starting along the marshland at the south end of Liberty Lake, this hike takes you through mixed forests, which consist of grand and Douglas fir, western hemlock, western red cedar, and several deciduous species, as well as three species of pines. Then you climb more than 1,200 feet to reach the Camp Hughes Cabin. Past the cabin the route descends, following abandoned roadbeds back to lake level. This route is open yearlong, and camping is permitted along it in places. However, the trailhead, campground, and the road leading to them is closed during the winter months.

Distance: 7.4-mile lollipop
Hiking time: 3.5-5 hours
Difficulty: Moderate, except for a 1.6-mile strenuous section
Trail surface: Dirt trail
Best season: Summer and fall
Other trail users: Mountain bikes are often ridden along this route. Stock is permitted on most of the return portion (west side) of the loop.
Canine compatibility: Leashed dogs permitted
Fees and permits: None for parking/hiking; fee charged for camping at Liberty Lake Regional Park
Schedule: Open 24/7

Maps: USGS Liberty Lake, Mica Peak; National Geographic Washington topo on CD-ROM, disk 4, covers the area and shows parts of the route. Check out the map on the reader board at the trailhead before you start hiking.
Trail contact: Spokane County Parks and Recreation, 404 N. Havana St., Spokane 99202; (509) 477-4730
Special considerations: The route follows abandoned roadbeds, except for the 1.6-mile section from the Liberty Creek Cedar Forest to Camp Hughes, which is a steep, narrow, rough, and eroded dirt singletrack. Be sure to take along a map—there are several unsigned junctions along this route.

Finding the trailhead: From exit 296 on I-90, drive south 0.2 mile to Appleway Avenue. Turn left (east) onto Appleway and go 0.9 mile to Molter Road. Turn right (south) onto Molter Road, following the small signs toward Liberty Lake Regional Park, and drive 1.1 miles to Valley Way. Turn left onto Valley Way and head east for 0.8 mile. The road turns right (south) and becomes Lakeside Road. Follow Lakeside Road for 1.6 miles to Zepher Road. Turn right onto Zepher Road and soon enter Liberty Lake Regional Park. You will reach the campground and trailhead 0.8 mile after turning onto Zepher Road. The trailhead is at the southwest corner of the campground. There is parking for several cars at the trailhead. The elevation at the trailhead is 2,060 feet. GPS: N47 37.855' / W117 03.512'

Note: If you plan to use the lower portion of this trail during winter or early spring (the higher country will probably be snowed in), the road from the park entrance booth to the campground may be closed. In this case, turn right at the entrance booth and drive a short distance to the parking area next to the playground equipment. From this parking area, walk south along the east side of the marshland on a path, passing a boardwalk that leads to a viewing platform. The path soon joins a service road, which leads to the campground and trailhead. The added distance is only about 0.2 mile.

The Hike

This hike begins and ends on Liberty Creek Trail. Liberty Creek Trail begins at the south end of Liberty Lake Regional Park Campground. Before you begin your hike on the broad, gravel trail, stop and read the reader board, then pass through a gate and head south. Slightly more than 0.1 mile from the trailhead, there is a path to the left. Hike straight ahead here, staying on the main trail. At the junction the trail surface becomes dirt.

Three-tenths of a mile from the trailhead, the loop portion of this hike begins at the junction with the Edith Hanson Cut-Off Trail. You can hike the loop in either direction, but this description is clockwise, so bear left (straight ahead to the south). Bikes are allowed on this side of the loop, but horses are not. The track climbs very gently, heading south-southeast through the mixed forest. The trail splits a little over 1.0 mile from the trailhead. Take the left fork and cross a wooden bridge over Split Creek. The trails quickly rejoin each other after crossing the creek. In the 1.0 mile from the Split Creek crossing to the Liberty Creek Cedar Forest, the route crosses a couple more small wooden bridges and traverses wet areas on a couple of sections of boardwalk. Liberty Creek Cedar Forest, at 2,500 feet elevation, is the end of the gentle, broad trail for a while. Take the time to read the informational signs about the cedar forest.

At the cedar forest bear right, cross a wooden bridge over the creek, and start the steepest part of this hike. In the next 0.3 mile, the narrow and steep trail makes eleven switchbacks, climbing to a viewpoint at 2,790 feet elevation. To the north, Liberty Lake dominates the view.

The track crosses a couple of tiny streams, which may be dry, after passing the viewpoint. Then you make a couple more switchbacks before crossing a wooden bridge just below a small waterfall. By the time you reach the bridge and waterfall, you are 3.1 miles from the trailhead and have climbed to 2,870 feet elevation. Past the waterfall the track continues to climb, and in the next 0.5 mile you make fourteen more switchbacks. Then you cross the creek on a wooden bridge. The trail then leaves the creek behind and continues to climb. You will soon cross an abandoned roadbed with a sign next to it that states "More Hiking." Continue straight ahead here and climb the short distance to the top of a rise, at 3,260 feet elevation. The tread then passes a side trail that leads a short distance to an outhouse, before you descend the last few steps to Camp Hughes.

Camp Hughes is at 3,250 feet elevation and 3.7 miles from Liberty Lake Regional Park. There is a small cabin with a fireplace and bunks at the camp. As of this writing, the bunks are in poor condition. There's a fire pit outside the cabin.

Next to the cabin the Edith Hanson Riding Trail turns left. You will be following the riding trail for the next 3.2 miles, so turn left and descend a short distance to a junction with an abandoned roadbed. This roadbed, which is open to stock, will serve as the trail much of the way back to the trailhead.

Turn left on the roadbed and start a very gentle downgrade. In 0.4 mile the broad trail crosses a tiny stream, and you begin to descend a little more steeply. The track crosses another small stream 1.0 mile farther along.

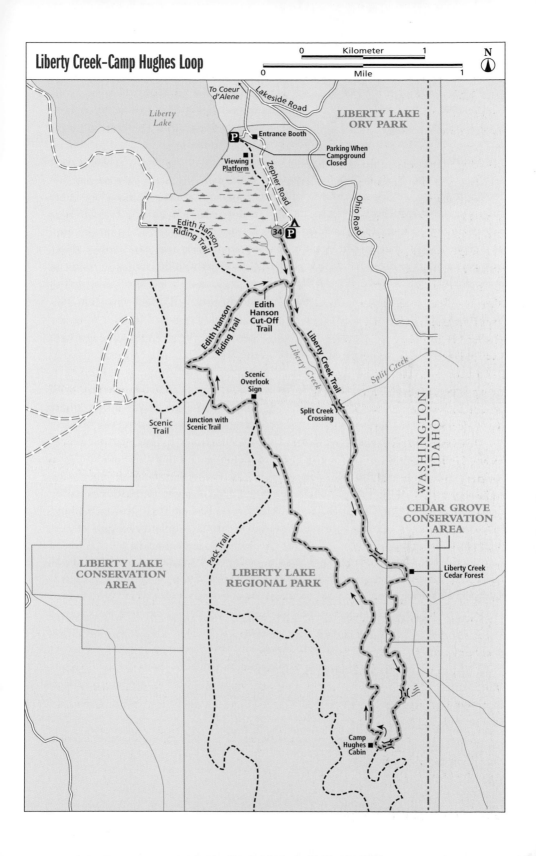

Liberty Creek-Camp Hughes Loop

0   Kilometer   1

0   Mile   1

N

Liberty Lake

To Coeur d'Alene

Lakeside Road

LIBERTY LAKE
ORV PARK

Entrance Booth

Parking When
Campground
Closed

Viewing
Platform

Zepher Road

Ohio Road

Edith Hanson
Riding Trail

Edith
Hanson
Cut-Off
Trail

Edith Hanson Riding Trail

Liberty Creek Trail

Liberty Creek

Split Creek

Scenic
Overlook
Sign

Split Creek
Crossing

WASHINGTON

IDAHO

Scenic
Trail

Junction with
Scenic Trail

CEDAR GROVE
CONSERVATION
AREA

LIBERTY LAKE
CONSERVATION
AREA

Pack Trail

LIBERTY LAKE
REGIONAL PARK

Liberty Creek
Cedar Forest

Camp
Hughes
Cabin

Waterfall next to the trail FRED BARSTAD

Another trail (abandoned road-bed) joins the one you are hiking on 2.0 miles from Camp Hughes. Continue straight ahead (northwest) here, descending gently. There are no signs at this junction.

You will reach a "Scenic Overlook" sign 0.1 mile after passing the unmarked junction; however, trees obstruct much of the view. There is another unmarked trail junction approximately 0.2 mile farther along. Bear slightly right, staying on the main trail, and walk a few yards downhill to the junction with the Scenic Trail. This signed junction is 6.0 miles from the starting trailhead. At the junction with the Scenic Trail, you have descended to 2,690 feet elevation.

After you pass the junction with the Scenic Trail, the tread continues straight ahead and descends moderately. Liberty Lake comes into view ahead, through the trees, 0.2 mile farther along.

The course passes through a gate and flattens out in another 0.5 mile. You soon reach the junction with the Edith Hanson Cut-Off Trail. A sign here commemorates Edith Hanson, for whom these trails were named. Hike straight ahead (northeast) on the Edith Hanson Cut-Off Trail. (The Edith Hanson Riding Trail turns to the left.) In a short distance the route turns to the east. You cross a couple of sluggish streams, then reach the junction with the Liberty Creek Trail, completing the loop. Turn left on the Liberty Creek Trail and retrace your steps the last 0.3 mile back to the trailhead.

Miles and Directions

0.0 Start at the Liberty Lake County Park and Trailhead and hike south.

0.3 Stay straight ahead at the trail junction to begin the loop.

2.1 Turn right at the Liberty Creek Cedar Forest and begin to climb.

3.1 The trail crosses a bridge below a waterfall.

3.7 Turn left at the Camp Hughes cabin onto the Edith Hanson Riding Trail.

6.0 Bear right at the junction with the Scenic Trail.

6.9 Hike straight ahead on the Edith Hanson Cut-Off Trail.

7.1 Turn left onto the Liberty Creek Trail.

7.4 Arrive back at the trailhead.

35 Columbia Plateau Trail

The section of the Columbia Plateau Trail described here is the only part of that trail that is currently paved. For kids that like trains, this is a great hike. You may get a close look at a train on a parallel track or crossing overhead on a bridge. This hike can be made one way, cutting the total distance in half, if a car shuttle to the Fish Lake Trailhead can be arranged. The Columbia Plateau Trail is a Rails-to-Trails project.

Distance: 7.6 miles out and back or 3.8-mile shuttle

Hiking time: About 3 hours out and back; 1.5 hours for shuttle

Difficulty: Easy

Trail surface: Paved path

Best season: Year-round, snow conditions permitting

Other trail users: The most common users of this section of the Columbia Plateau Trail are bicyclists. Horses and motorized vehicles are prohibited. This portion of the Columbia Plateau Trail is accessible for people with physical challenges.

Canine compatibility: Dogs must be kept on a leash, which is very important for safety here because of the numbers of bicyclists.

Fees and permits: Discover Pass required for parking at the trailhead

Schedule: Year-round

Maps: The map in this book is more than adequate for this hike. Many maps show this route as a railroad track, which it once was.

Trail contact: The Columbia Plateau Trail is currently managed by Riverside State Park, 9711 W. Charles Rd., Nine Mile Falls 99026; (509) 465-5064; parks.state.wa.us/573/Riverside

Special considerations: Even though pedestrians have the right-of-way over bicyclists, it is always a good idea to be courteous and move to the side to allow them to pass safely.

Finding the trailhead: From downtown Spokane, take I-90 west for 11 miles to exit 270. Take the exit and drive south for 6 miles on WA 904 to Cheney. Drive south from Cheney on the Cheney-Spangle Road for 1 mile. The parking area and trailhead are on the left side of the road. Shaded picnic tables and restrooms are available at the trailhead, but there's no water. The trailhead is at 2,300 feet elevation. GPS: N47 28.767' / W117 33.652'

The Hike

At the northwest corner of the parking area, descend the paved path for a few yards to the Columbia Plateau Trail and turn right. A sign informs you here that it is 0.25 mile to the Water Station and 3.75 miles to the Fish Lake Trailhead. The actual distances are slightly farther in both cases. Other signs let you know that the maximum speed is 15 mph for bicycles and that you are entering the city of Cheney. The route leads northwest following the old railroad grade through a cut rimmed with aspen and ponderosa pine trees.

Three-tenths of a mile from the trailhead, you pass mile marker 361. The mile markers are the distances from Portland, Oregon, along the old railroad. On the left,

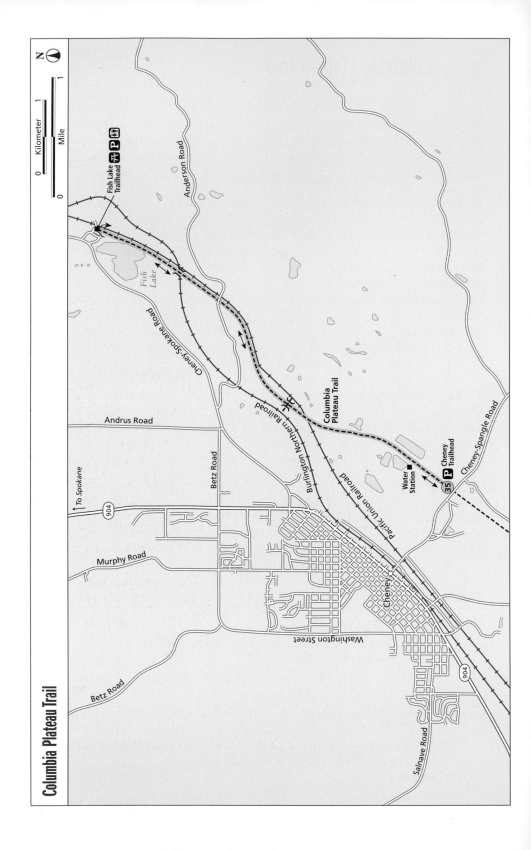

Columbia Plateau Trail

Fish Lake Trailhead [P] [♿]

Anderson Road

Fish Lake

Cheney-Spokane Road

Andrus Road

Betz Road

To Spokane

904

Murphy Road

Betz Road

Burlington Northern Railroad

Columbia Plateau Trail

Pacific Union Railroad

Water Station

Cheney Trailhead 35 [P]

Cheney-Spangle Road

Washington Street

Cheney

Salnave Road

904

N

0   Kilometer   1
0   Mile   1

Columbia Plateau Trail FRED BARSTAD

0.1 mile past the mile marker, you reach the Water Station, which has a shaded bench and a fountain. As you pass the Water Station, the course enters a more open area. For about 0.2 mile the broad, paved trail traverses open country. Then, as the route passes through a cut in the layered basalt, trees show up again. A sluggish stream follows the grade through the cut. Muskrats are occasionally seen in this stream.

The track leaves the city of Cheney 1.1 miles from the trailhead. Soon the tread passes mile marker 362, then goes beneath a railroad overpass. The trail goes under a wooden bridge 0.2 mile farther along. The trail leaves the cut about 2.0 miles from the trailhead. Past the cut there is a field and a house to the left of the trail. To your right is a railroad track. The route passes mile marker 363 before long, then enters another cut. The Anderson Road Bridge crosses overhead, 2.7 miles from the Cheney Trailhead.

Four-tenths of a mile farther along, the trail passes beneath another railroad bridge and reaches mile marker 364 in another 0.2 mile. Fish Lake comes into view to the left just past the mile marker. The Fish Lake Trailhead is reached slightly more than 3.8 miles from the Cheney Trailhead. If you haven't arranged a car shuttle, turn around here and retrace your steps to the Cheney Trailhead.

Miles and Directions

0.0 Start at the Cheney Trailhead; descend the path and turn right.

0.4 Pass the Water Station.

3.8 Reach the Fish Lake Trailhead. If you haven't arranged for a car shuttle, turn around and retrace your steps to the Cheney Trailhead.

7.6 Arrive back at the Cheney Trailhead.

36 Iller Creek Conservation Area

This low-elevation loop right outside Spokane leads through a pleasant forest to tall granite cliffs and views over the rolling green Palouse country. The granite cliffs will surprise you by appearing as you round a bend on the trail. From the top of a rocky ridge, you'll descend among grass and flowers back toward the Spokane Valley.

Distance: 5.0-mile loop
Hiking time: About 2.5 hours
Difficulty: Easy due to distance and gentle terrain
Trail surface: Dirt trail
Best season: Spring and fall; also a popular winter snowshoe route
Other trail users: Mountain bikers

Canine compatibility: Leashed dogs permitted
Fees and permits: No fees or permits required
Schedule: Open 24/7
Map: USGS Spokane SE
Trail contact: Spokane County Parks and Recreation Department; (509) 477-4730
Special considerations: This hike includes an elevation gain of 1,125 feet.

Finding the trailhead: From I-90 take exit 287 for Argonne Road. Go south on Argonne Road for 1.5 miles, at which point you pass Sprague Street and Argonne Road becomes South Dishman Mica Road. In about 2 miles turn right onto Schafer Road at a stoplight. At a stop sign in 0.9 mile, turn right (east) onto 44th Avenue. In 0.2 mile turn left onto Farr Road and continue 0.3 mile to a stop sign. Turn right (east) onto Holman Road and continue 0.7 mile to a hairpin turn. Park on the shoulder outside the gate to the Iller Creek Conservation Area. GPS: N 47 36.10' / W 117 16.90'

The Hike

This loop hike through a conservation area outside Spokane is convenient and varied. The trailhead is barely outside the urban area but quickly leads deep into the forest to a ridge full of towering granite crags. These crags, called the Rocks of Sharon, jut straight up and lean out toward the Palouse country to the south, a lowland plain of rolling green hills. It's the perfect forest for a quick wilderness escape.

This trail loops through most of the 876-acre Iller Creek Conservation Area. The area is part of the larger Dishman Hills Conservation Area, which is managed by Spokane County Parks, the state Department of Natural Resources, and the Dishman Hills Conservancy.

These naked rocks and their huge prominence are amplified by the gentle terrain of the rolling Palouse wheat fields far below. From the trail by Rocks of Sharon, you can see south out over the plain to Steptoe and Kamiak Buttes, the two tallest humps on the horizon. These hills are about 50 miles away. It's a perfect vantage for enjoying the big sky of eastern Washington. Along the trail you can also see the wide Spokane Valley and the Selkirk Mountains in Idaho to the east.

Big Rock and the Palouse Region OLIVER LAZENBY

Enter the gate at the trailhead and bear right at the junction, staying on the west side of the creek. A mixed forest of pines and firs lines the trail. Thimbleberries and currants make up much of the understory. This path is wide and easy to follow, even in winter. The trip to Rocks of Sharon is a popular snowshoe trek. At 1.7 miles from the trailhead, bear right at a junction. The trail to the left makes a shorter loop, but it doesn't go all the way to the hilltop views.

Two miles from the trailhead you'll be walking through a lush forest that resembles western Washington, when suddenly the Rocks of Sharon appear. Stroll beneath the monoliths along a high ridge littered with granite. The bigger rock faces are to the right of the trail. The biggest of the crags, simply named Big Rock, is more than 200 feet tall.

The views don't end at Big Rock. From the hike's high point at 2.3 miles, the trail winds to the north and begins descending on an open ridge covered in phlox, balsamroot, lupine, and other wildflowers. Take in views of the Spokane Valley and the forest that surrounds you as you make your way slowly down the trail. The views don't cease until you begin switchbacking downhill toward the creek, 0.5 mile from the parking lot.

Iller Creek Conservation Area

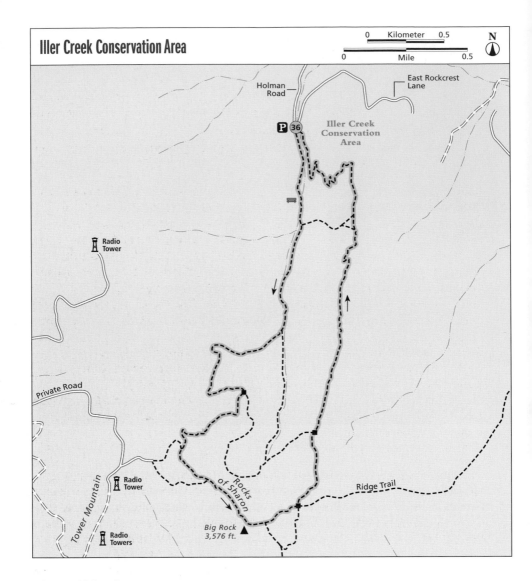

0 Kilometer 0.5

0 Mile 0.5

N

Holman Road

East Rockcrest Lane

P 36

Iller Creek Conservation Area

Radio Tower

Private Road

Radio Tower

Tower Mountain

Radio Towers

Rocks of Sharon

Big Rock 3,576 ft.

Ridge Trail

Miles and Directions

0.0   Start at the trailhead on Holman Road; stay right at the fork.

0.3   Pass a bench on the side of the trail.

1.7   Stay right at a junction with a cutoff trail for the shorter loop.

2.3   Pass the Rocks of Sharon to the right (south) of the trail; 0.2 mile later you'll pass the remains of a red pickup truck.

2.9   Bear left at a junction with a small trail.

3.2   Bear right at a junction with the shorter loop trail.

5.0   Arrive back at the trailhead.

37 Centennial Trail

Hike the paved Centennial Trail from the Sontag Park Trailhead near Nine Mile Falls through Riverside State Park to the Military Cemetery Trailhead. This is the most scenic part of the 37-mile-long Centennial Trail and the section that is best adapted to hikers. Allow plenty of time to enjoy the viewpoints overlooking the sometimes calm, sometimes frothing Spokane River.

Distance: 9.4-mile shuttle

Hiking time: About 5 hours

Difficulty: Easy

Trail surface: Paved path

Best season: Spring through fall; also winter, depending on snow conditions

Other trail users: Bicyclists are the most common users of the Centennial Trail. This entire trail is accessible by people with physical challenges.

Canine compatibility: Leashed dogs permitted. Be extra careful with your pet due to bicycle traffic.

Fees and permits: Discover Pass required

Schedule: Year-round, dawn to dusk

Maps: *Washington State Parks Riverside State Park* brochure and map, available for free at state park headquarters and the Bowl and Pitches campground entrance. Riverside State Park Multiuse Trail Map, produced by the Inland Empire Backcountry Horsemen, PO Box 30891, Spokane 99223; www.iebch.com; map may be purchased at the state park. National Geographic Washington topo map on CD-ROM, disk 4. Montana Mapping & GPS LLC's hunting and GPS maps, available at www.huntinggps maps.com.

Trail contact: Riverside State Park, 9711 Charles Rd., Nine Mile Falls 99026; (509) 465-5064; riversidestatepark.org

Special considerations: Watch for fast bicycle traffic, especially on hills and blind corners.

Finding the trailhead: There are many ways to reach this trailhead; this is a route from the center of Spokane. Take Division Street north from I-90 to Francis, which is WA 291. Turn left onto Francis and follow it to 9-Mile Road, also WA 291. Bear right on 9-Mile Road and drive northwest for 6.3 miles to Charles Road. Turn left and cross the bridge over the Spokane River below Nine Mile Falls Dam. Follow Charles Road for 0.3 mile to the Sontag Park Trailhead. The park and trailhead are on the right side of Charles Road. GPS: N47 46.686' / W117 32.966'

To reach the Military Cemetery Trailhead, where this hike ends, return to 9-Mile Road, turn right and drive south to 7-Mile Road. Turn right and follow 7-Mile Road to Inland Road. Turn left onto Inland Road and follow it and Old Trails Road south to Government Way. Turn left onto Government Way and drive to the trailhead, which is a short distance off Government Way, on your left. The Washington State Parks Riverside State Park brochure and map is helpful when trying to find the Military Cemetery Trailhead.

The Hike

The Centennial Trail leads south from the Sontag Park Trailhead, quickly crossing Charles Road. After crossing Charles Road the route follows Carlson Road. This section of the Centennial Trail is shared with motorized traffic, so watch for cars. After

Spokane River FRED BARSTAD

climbing gently for 0.7 mile, the route makes a left turn, leaving Carlson Road. The track here becomes, for now, a nonmotorized route. You will reach the junction with Trail 400, which is to the right, 0.5 mile after leaving Carlson Road. Another 0.3 mile brings you to the junction with Trail 411. If you would like to make a side trip, Trail 411 climbs to your right, reaching some interesting lava formations in a short distance.

After passing the junction with Trail 411, the Centennial Trail crosses the Deep Creek Bridge and begins to climb toward the junction with State Park Drive. The junction is reached in a little less than 0.7 mile after climbing about 90 feet in elevation, through mostly Douglas fir woods. State Park Drive is closed to unauthorized motor vehicles and is a popular biking and hiking route. To your right on State Park Drive, it's only a short side hike of about 0.4 mile to Deep Creek Overlook. The view from the overlook includes the rugged Deep Creek Canyon and the chaotic lava lands across it.

Leaving the junction with State Park Drive, the route continues southeast, passing beneath some power lines and reaching the McLellan Trailhead in 0.6 mile. Past the trailhead the route is again a road that is shared with motorized traffic. You pass some houses next to the road and in about 0.5 mile cross 7-Mile Road. For the next 0.7 mile, the route is still shared with cars, and then you reach the Wilber Road Trailhead. A short distance after passing the Wilber Road Trailhead, the 25-Mile Trail crosses the

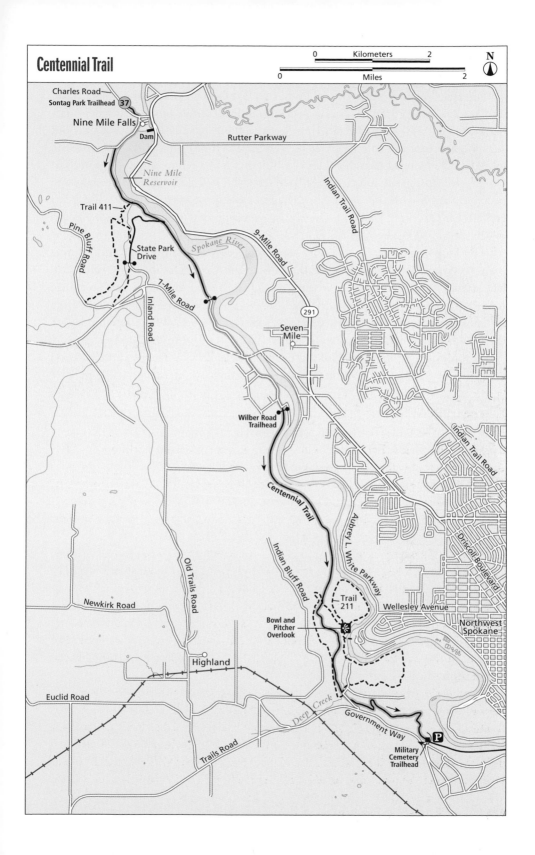

Kilometers

0   2

Miles

0   2

N

Charles Road—
Sontag Park Trailhead 37

Nine Mile Falls

Dam

Rutter Parkway

Nine Mile
Reservoir

Trail 411

Pine Bluff Road

State Park
Drive

Spokane River

Inland Road

7-Mile Road

9-Mile Road

Indian Trail Road

291

Seven
Mile

Wilber Road
Trailhead

Centennial Trail

Indian Trail Road

Old Trails Road

Indian Bluff Road

Aubrey L. White Parkway

Driscoll Boulevard

Newkirk Road

Trail
211

Wellesley Avenue

Northwest
Spokane

Bowl and
Pitcher
Overlook

Highland

Euclid Road

Deep Creek

Government Way

P

Military
Cemetery
Trailhead

Trails Road

Centennial Trail. Shortly thereafter there is a fireplace and a kiosk with information about it to the right of the trail.

You reach the first junction with Trail 211 1.3 miles after passing the Wilber Road Trailhead. Continue southeast on the paved trail for 0.5 mile more to another junction with Trail 211. To the left Trail 211 leads to the Bowl and Pitcher area in about 1.0 mile. Stay on the Centennial Trail, heading south. In 0.7 mile Trail 210 crosses the route. The Centennial Trail then climbs a little before flattening out. Eight-tenths of a mile after passing the junction with Trail 210, you will pass a gate. Here the route becomes shared with cars again. Shortly after passing the gate, you reach the Bowl and Pitcher Overlook Trailhead. There is an excellent view from here looking down on the Bowl and Pitcher formation in the Spokane River.

The broad, paved track continues south after passing the overlook. In 0.4 mile there is a junction with the road to the Equestrian Area. In another 100 yards turn left, leaving the shared road. Now the Centennial Trail heads southeast. The course makes a descending S turn 0.3 mile ahead. Stay to the edge of the trail here and watch for bicycle traffic on these nearly blind corners. Past the S turn the route heads east, then south, reaching the Military Cemetery Trailhead in another 1.2 miles.

This is by no means the end of the Centennial Trail, but it is a good place to end your hike. Much of the rest of the trail is through the city.

Miles and Directions

- **0.0** Start at the Sontag Park Trailhead and head south.
- **1.5** Pass the junction with Trail 411.
- **2.2** Pass the junction with State Park Drive.
- **3.3** The route crosses 7-Mile Road.
- **4.0** Pass the Wilber Road Trailhead.
- **5.8** Pass Trail 211 for the second time.
- **7.4** Pass the Bowl and Pitcher Overlook Trailhead.
- **9.4** Arrive at the Military Cemetery Trailhead.

38 Entrance Loop

Hike along the abandoned dirt roadbeds that make up the Entrance Loop through widely diverse second-growth forest. The route is never very steep, is wide all the way, and has no cliffs close to it, making it an excellent hike with children.

Distance: 1.4-mile loop
Hiking time: About 1 hour
Difficulty: Easy
Trail surface: Dirt trail; old roadbeds
Best season: Late spring, summer, and fall for hiking; a great snowshoe trail in winter
Other trail users: These trails are open to bicyclists and equestrians during the summer season. In winter Entrance Loop is used as a snowshoe route. Snowmobiles may only use the 0.3-mile-long Trail 120 section of this loop.
Canine compatibility: Dogs must be on a leash and under physical control at all times. Be wary of bicycle traffic.
Fees and permits: Discover Pass required; Sno-Park permit required during winter
Schedule: Year-round, dawn to dusk
Maps: The Mount Spokane State Park map produced by Washington State Parks, with donated proceeds made when renewing motor vehicle licenses, is free and adequate for the less-complicated hikes like this one. Dharma-maps's Mount Spokane State Park map is a good topo of the state park that shows all the trails. Montana Mapping & GPS LLC's hunting and GPS maps are good topos of the area, as are National Geographic maps on CD-ROM; however, neither of these shows all the trails.
Trail contact: Mount Spokane State Park, 26107 N. Mount Spokane Park Dr., Mead 99021; (509) 238-4258; e-mail: mount .spokane@parks.wa.gov
Special considerations: Expect snow in winter. Keep an eye out for snowmobiles on the Trail 120 portion of this hike (snowshoe) during winter.

Finding the trailhead: From downtown Spokane, head north on Division Street to the junction with US 2 (Newport Highway). Follow US 2 to the junction with WA 206 (Mount Spokane Park Drive). Turn right on WA 206 and drive 15.3 miles to the Mount Spokane State Park entrance. Pass the entrance and go another 0.3 mile to the Entrance Loop Trailhead. Parking and restrooms are on the left side of the road. This hike begins across the road from the parking area, at 3,230 feet elevation. GPS: N47 53.292' / W117 07.510'

The Hike

After crossing the highway, begin your hike up Trail 122. Of the two trails that depart from this trailhead, Trail 122 is the one on the right. Your return trail (121) is the trail to left. The route climbs moderately to the south-southwest as you leave the trailhead.

Douglas fir, western larch, western red cedar, and western hemlock as well as grand fir shadow the course, with Rocky Mountain maple, aka Douglas maple, providing an understory in the more open spots.

Soon the route makes a turn to the left (southeast). About 0.5 mile from the trailhead, you reach the junction with Trail 120. At the junction you have climbed to 3,580 feet elevation. Turn left at the junction and head easterly on Trail 120. For the

Entrance Loop Trail FRED BARSTAD

0.3 mile to the junction with Trail 121, the course remains at about that elevation. Trail 120 continues to the trailhead and parking area next to the junction of Mount Spokane Park Drive and Mount Spokane Summit Road. See "Option" below.

GRAND FIR

Generally found at low to middle elevations, the grand fir (*Abies grandis*) is a large conifer, reaching 140 feet or more in height. One of the keys to identifying the grand fir is its needles, which are arranged in two rows opposite each other on the branch. The dark green needles also have a notch in the tip. The grand fir is also called white fir in most of the Northwest. This is a reference to its light-colored wood, as compared to the red heartwood of the Douglas fir, which is often referred to as red fir in the inland Northwest. The light green cones on the grand fir's upper branches are 3 or 4 inches long. Like with other true firs (*Abies*), the cones stand erect from the twigs.

The wood of the grand fir is not highly valued as lumber, but it is often used for plywood and chipboard. Its value as firewood cannot be underrated, as it provides limited heat and lots of ash.

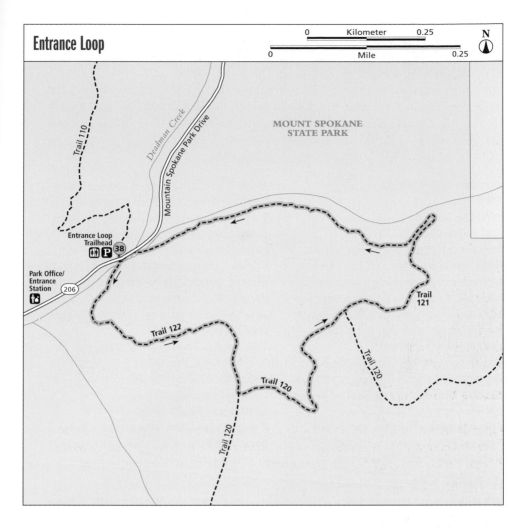

Entrance Loop

Turn left onto Trail 121 and descend to the north. Soon the trail makes a wide switchback to the left and crosses a tiny stream. There is a larger stream on the right side of the trail after you pass the switchback. The route soon crosses another small stream, which passes beneath the abandoned roadbed in a culvert. As you hike the last part of the route back to the Entrance Loop Trailhead, bracken fern lines much of the course.

Miles and Directions

0.0 Cross the highway and hike south-southwest (counterclockwise) on Trail 122.

0.5 Turn left at the junction onto Trail 120.

0.8 Turn left again at the junction onto Trail 121.

1.4 Arrive back at the Entrance Loop Trailhead. *Option:* This hike can be combined with Trail 120 to make an 8.2-mile lollipop loop from the snowmobile Sno-Park parking area next to the junction of Mount Spokane Park Drive and Mount Spokane Summit Road.

39 Mount Kit Carson–Day Mountain Loop

First climb the moderately steep Trail 110, gaining over 1,600 feet of elevation. Then follow the Mount Kit Carson Loop Road (which is closed to unauthorized motorized traffic) as it descends very gradually through the diverse mountain forest, before retracing your steps for the last 1.8 miles to the Entrance Loop Trailhead. Watch for the fairly common white-tailed deer all along this hike.

Distance: 12.0-mile lollipop
Hiking time: 4.5–7 hours
Difficulty: Moderate to strenuous
Trail surface: Dirt trail
Best seasons: Summer and early fall
Other trail users: These trails are open to bicyclists and equestrians during summer. Mountain bikers are the most common users of the Mount Kit Carson Loop Road portion of this hike. In winter snowshoers and cross-country skiers use the route.
Canine compatibility: Dogs must be on a leash and under physical control at all times. Beware of cyclists, and keep your pet far away from horses to avoid spooking them.
Fees and permits: Discover Pass required; Sno-Park permit required during winter
Schedule: Year-round, dawn to dusk.

Maps: Dharmamaps's Mount Spokane State Park is an up-to-date topo of the state park. The Mount Spokane State Park map produced by Washington State Parks, with donated proceeds made when renewing motor vehicle licenses, is free and available at the state park entrance. Montana Mapping & GPS LLC's hunting and GPS maps are good topos of the area, as is the National Geographic Washington topo map on CD-ROM, disk 4.
Trail contact: Mount Spokane State Park, 26107 N. Mount Spokane Park Dr., Mead 99021; (509) 238-4258; e-mail: mount .spokane@parks.wa.gov
Special considerations: Expect snow in winter. A small portion of this route crosses private timberland. Please stay on the route (roadbed) in that area (it is clear-cut).

Finding the trailhead: From downtown Spokane, head north on Division Street to the junction with US 2 (Newport Highway). Follow US 2 northeast to the junction with WA 206 (Mount Spokane Park Drive). Turn right on WA 206 and drive 15.3 miles to the Mount Spokane State Park entrance, where you must stop. Pass the entrance and go another 0.3 mile to the Entrance Loop Trailhead. Parking and restrooms are on the left side of the road. This hike begins from the parking area, at 3,230 feet elevation. There is a sign marking Trail 110. GPS: N47 53.288' / W117 07.540'

The Hike

Trail 110 heads north, climbing rather steeply, from the Entrance Loop Trailhead. Grand fir, western red cedar, aspen, and Rocky Mountain maple line the track as you ascend. One-eighth of a mile from the trailhead, the course makes four switchbacks as you pass some fairly large Douglas firs. Above the switchbacks the tread passes beneath power lines. Soon the grade moderates and some western white pines and hemlocks show up next to the trail. Grouse can often be seen along this part of the route.

Soon the trail descends slightly and passes mile marker 0.5, at 3,570 feet elevation. You will reach a trail junction 0.1 mile after passing the marker post. Bear slightly right at the junction on what is now a dirt roadbed, lined in places with goldenrod. The area to the left (west) here is closed to entry. The course crosses through a saddle at 3,540 feet elevation a little more than 0.1 mile past the junction. Then you climb gently through the forest, which now includes western larch and lodgepole pine trees, to another trail junction. Bear left here—the trail to the right also enters an area that is closed to entry. These side trails are not shown on Dharmamaps's *Mount Spokane State Park* map.

The route crosses a tiny stream, which flows beneath it in a culvert, and reaches mile marker 1.0, 0.2 mile after passing the junction. Soon after passing mile marker 1.0, Mount Spokane Park Drive comes into view to the right. The trail parallels the highway for about 0.25 mile, then bears left, leaving it. Before long the trace reaches mile marker 1.5 as you hike through a forest that is now nearly devoid of undergrowth. You will cross fern-lined Burping Brook 0.1 mile past mile marker 1.5. A little more hiking brings you to the first junction with the Mount Kit Carson Loop Road. The track passes a restroom and a table just before reaching the junction. The Mount Kit Carson Loop Road is closed to unauthorized motor vehicle access. This junction, at 3,800 feet elevation, is 1.8 miles from the Entrance Loop Trailhead.

This is the beginning of the loop portion of this hike. Cross the Mount Kit Carson Loop Road and climb through the cedar and hemlock forest, staying on Trail 110. This section of Trail 110 is marked with blue diamond cross-country ski and snowshoe markers. The track makes three switchbacks before reaching the junction with Trail 100. Turn left at the junction. Trails 110 and 100 follow the same route for the next 0.3 mile. You reach the trail junction where Trails 100 and 110 separate again, at about 4,100 feet elevation, after passing mile marker 2.0. Turn right at this junction and continue to climb on Trail 110, quickly crossing a tiny stream. Bracken fern lines the route through the open woods as you pass mile marker 2.5.

The course makes a wide switchback to the left 0.1 mile after passing mile marker 2.5. A couple tenths of a mile farther along, the track crosses a tiny stream. Soon thimbleberry bushes crowd the trail. As you cross another small stream a little farther along, monkshood joins the mix of flowers. Soon the trail bears left, leaving the long-abandoned roadbed that it has been following for some time. You pass mile marker 3 at about 4,450 feet elevation. Here huckleberry bushes and bear grass grow between the very old stumps that dot the forest floor beneath the medium-age trees.

The trail makes three more switchbacks before reaching mile marker 3.5 at 4,720 feet elevation. Soon you make yet another switchback, then climb the last third of a mile to another junction with the Mount Kit Carson Loop Road at Saddle Junction. Besides the loop road, Trails 140, 130, and 170 meet at Saddle Junction. There is also a restroom here. The forest at the junction has become more subalpine in character, with a mix of subalpine fir, western larch, lodgepole pine, and western white pine. Beneath the trees a few mountain ash and lots of huckleberry bushes cover the ground. This junction, at 4,870 feet elevation, is 4.3 miles from the Entrance Loop Trailhead.

Pearly everlasting FRED BARSTAD

Turn left at Saddle Junction and hike northwest on the wide, dirt and gravel Mount Kit Carson Loop Road. The track descends very gently, and in slightly less than 0.5 mile you pass mile marker 5.0. These markers are for the Mount Kit Carson Loop Road and not a continuation of the markers on Trail 110, although the distance seems to almost match. Look to your right between here and mile marker 4.5 for a view of the summit area of Mount Spokane and the towers atop it. You will reach the junction with Trail 130 0.1 mile after passing the 4.5-mile marker. Trail 130, which is to the right at this junction, is also known as Chair Road. Trail 130 follows the Mount Kit Carson Loop Road for a short distance to the northwest and then leaves the loop by climbing steeply to the left.

Hike straight ahead at the junction, staying on the Mount Kit Carson Loop Road. In a short distance the route leaves Mount Spokane State Park and enters land owned by the Inland Empire Paper Company. This area was nearly clear-cut several years ago, so the view is good. Stay on the roadbed while on the private land. In 0.7 mile the course reenters Mount Spokane State Park and you are back in the timber again. There is a trail (road) junction 0.3 mile after reentering the state park. Hike straight ahead, staying on the Mount Kit Carson Loop Road, and soon pass mile marker 3.5.

The route crosses Little Deer Creek 0.4 mile after passing mile marker 3.5. Next to the creek is a table, which makes this a good spot to stop for a snack or lunch. Soon after crossing Little Deer Creek, you pass mile marker 3.0. Continue southwest, then

Sore paws means hitching a ride back to the trailhead.

south along the Mount Kit Carson Loop Road, passing mile markers 2.5 and 2.0. Shortly after mile marker 2.0, there is another table next to the tread as you cross a small stream. You will reach the junction with Day Road 0.25 mile farther along. This junction, at 3,950 feet elevation, is 8.6 miles into the hike. Hike straight ahead at the junction, staying on the Mount Kit Carson Loop Road.

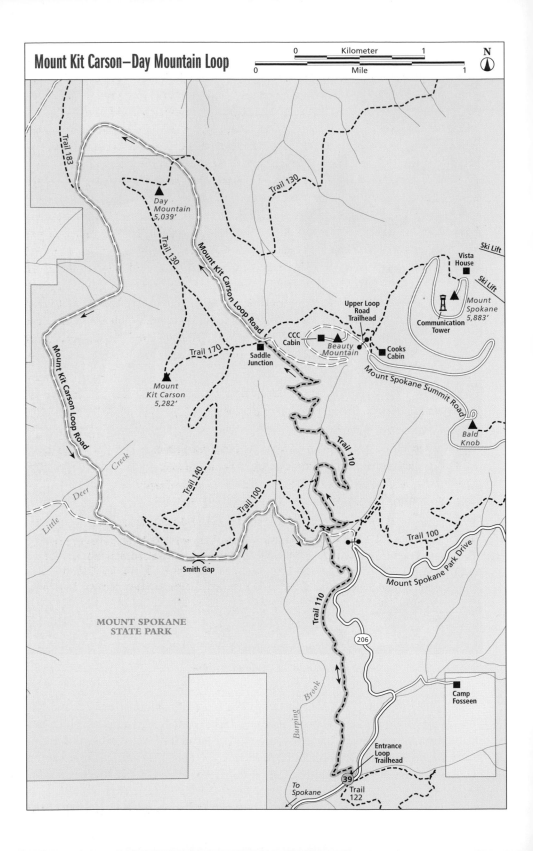

Mount Kit Carson–Day Mountain Loop

Kilometer
0   1
Mile
0   1

N

Trail 183

Day Mountain
5,039'

Trail 130

Trail 130

Mount Kit Carson Loop Road

Trail 130

Mount Kit Carson Loop Road

Trail 170

Saddle Junction

CCC Cabin

Upper Loop Road Trailhead

Beauty Mountain

Cooks Cabin

Vista House

Ski Lift

Ski Lift

Mount Spokane
5,883'

Communication Tower

Mount Spokane Summit Road

Mount Kit Carson
5,282'

Trail 140

Trail 100

Bald Knob

Trail 110

Creek

Deer

Little

Smith Gap

Trail 110

Trail 100

Mount Spokane Park Drive

206

MOUNT SPOKANE
STATE PARK

Camp Fosseen

Burping Brook

Trail 110

Entrance Loop Trailhead

To Spokane

39

Trail 122

Soon the track passes mile marker 1.5 and reaches another junction. The trail (roadbed) to the right is Trail 155. The junction with Trail 155 is 0.3 mile from the junction with Day Road. Hike straight ahead (east southeast), staying on the Mount Kit Carson Loop Road. A few yards after passing the junction with Trail 155, Trail 140 leaves the loop road to the right. Hike straight ahead. Shortly after passing the junction with Trail 140, Trail 100 turns off to the left. Hike straight ahead a few more yards to Smith Gap and another junction with Trail 140. Smith Gap, where you will find a table and a restroom, is at 4,170 feet elevation, 9.1 miles from where you started at the Entrance Loop Trailhead. You have 2.9 miles left to go to complete the hike.

Bear slightly left at the junction with Trail 140, staying on the Mount Kit Carson Loop Road, and begin to descend as you hike east–northeast. In 0.25 mile you will pass mile marker 1.0. Mount Spokane is now almost directly ahead. In about 0.2 mile the route passes another table next to a tiny stream. You will cross another small stream before reaching mile marker 0.5. In another 0.3 mile you reach the junction with a short connector trail that goes to Trail 100. Stay on the Mount Kit Carson Loop Road, heading east, and quickly reach the junction with Trail 110, where the loop portion of this hike started. Turn right onto Trail 110 and retrace your steps, descending for 1.8 miles to the Entrance Loop Trailhead.

Miles and Directions

0.0   Start at the Entrance Loop Trailhead and climb north.

1.8   Cross Mount Kit Carson Loop Road.

4.3   At Saddle Junction turn left on the Mount Kit Carson Loop Road.

5.4   At the junction with Trail 130 (Chair Road), hike straight ahead.

8.6   At the junction with Day Road, hike straight ahead to the southeast.

9.1   Cross Smith Gap. Hike slightly left, heading east-northeast.

10.2   Return to the junction of Mount Kit Carson Loop Road and Trail 110; turn right.

12.0   Arrive back at the Entrance Loop Trailhead. *Option:* This hike could be shortened by more than 3 miles by starting and ending at the Lower Loop Road Trailhead, approximately 0.2 mile east along Mount Kit Carson Loop Road from its lower junction with Trail 110. To reach the Lower Loop Road Trailhead, drive another 1.6 miles northeast, then north along WA 206 from the Entrance Loop Trailhead.

40 Sherman Peak Loop

Sunshine, high lumpy mountains, larches, and views spanning Washington's east side from the Cascades to the Selkirk Mountains are the highlights of the loop hike around Sherman Peak. From a high, paved trailhead, it doesn't take long to get to some of the best views in the Kettle River Range. And there is a bonus along the way: a rustic cabin where pups are welcome overnight!

Distance: 6.1-mile lollipop
Hiking time: About 3.5 hours
Difficulty: Moderate due to elevation gain and distance
Trail surface: Dirt trail
Best season: July–Oct
Other trail users: Equestrians, mountain bikers
Canine compatibility: Dogs must be leashed when in or around developed recreation sites, trailheads, interpretive trails, or campgrounds; voice control allowed in forest and wilderness areas. Always check at the trailhead for specific information regarding leash vs. voice control regulations.
Fees and permits: No fees or permits required
Schedule: Open 24/7
Map: USGS Sherman Peak, Copper Butte
Trail contact: Colville National Forest, Republic Ranger District; (509) 775-7400
Special considerations: This hike includes an elevation gain of 1,100 feet.

Finding the trailhead: From Tonasket drive east on US 20 for 40 miles. Turn right onto Clark Avenue in downtown Republic to stay on US 20. Continue 16.6 miles to the top of Sherman Pass to an access road going north, with a sign for recreational opportunities. Continue 0.1 mile to a parking lot. Alternately, reach Sherman Pass from Kettle Falls by driving 26.3 miles west on US 20. GPS: N48 36.48' / W118 28.63'

The Hike

Between the North Cascades and the Selkirks, a high, lonely mountain range called the Kettle River Range stretches into Canada. The range runs north to south between the towns of Republic and Kettle Falls and is intersected by US 20 at Sherman Pass, the highest paved mountain pass in the state. The Kettles are tall, remote, and supremely quiet. Even the trailhead for the Sherman Peak Loop, the easiest in the range to reach, is lonely.

Sherman Peak, a lofty mountain just south of Sherman Pass, is one of the taller peaks in the southern end of the Kettle Crest Range. A relatively easy trail loops around the peak, affording incredible views of the Kettles. At the southern end of the loop, the trail joins the Kettle Crest Trail, which roams north–south along the spine of the Kettles for about 45 miles. Some hikers climb Sherman Peak off-trail from the south end of the loop. The trail around the mountain offers views in all directions because much of the forest burned during the 1988 White Mountain Fire. Vegetation along the Sherman Peak Loop alternates between forest and charred areas quickly growing up with young larches and lodgepole pines.

Snow Peak Cabin, 1.4 miles from Sherman Peak OLIVER LAZENBY

From the parking lot, the trail dips into a narrow drainage before climbing back toward US 20. When you get to the road, look for the other end of the trail just uphill. It's hidden from sight behind a boulder. Next you'll switchback uphill for 0.7 mile to the junction with the loop trail. Turn right (west) and come out of the forest into an open, burned area called Gleason's Gallop. Just downhill, the larches are tall and abundant. They seem to turn gold a little later than larches in the Cascades. In season, this is a fantastic spot to watch the delicate needles change color before falling off.

Brittle, sun-bleached snags stand throughout this area and litter the ground. They frequently blow down, so expect to climb over and under some logs on this hike. The Sherman Loop Trail joins the Kettle Crest Trail 3.1 miles from the trailhead. Bear left to continue the loop, or go right to hike beneath Snow Peak and explore the Kettle Crest Trail toward the Snow Peak Cabin. The forest service and several clubs completed the cozy log cabin in 1995 after several years of work. You can reserve the cabin for a reasonable nightly fee.

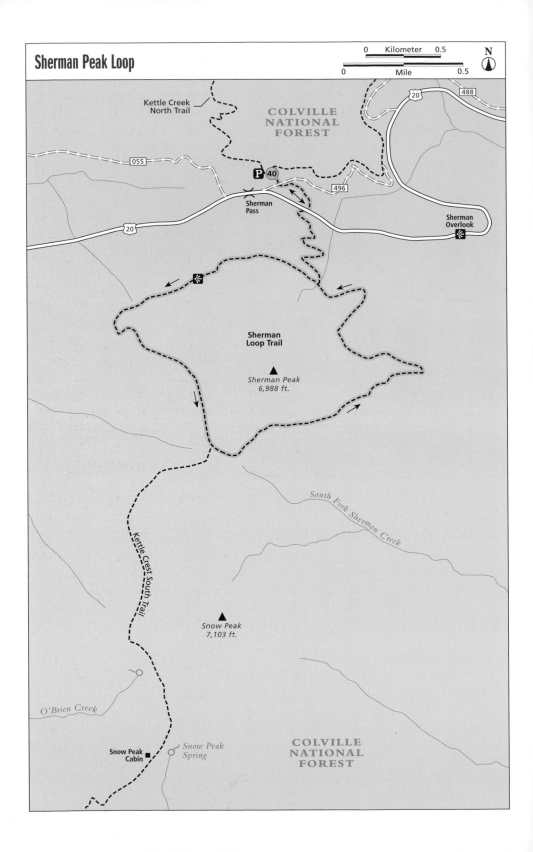

Sherman Peak Loop

Kettle Creek
North Trail

COLVILLE
NATIONAL
FOREST

0   Kilometer   0.5

0   Mile   0.5

N

20

488

055

P 40

496

Sherman
Pass

20

Sherman
Overlook

Sherman
Loop Trail

Sherman Peak
6,988 ft.

South Fork Shermon Creek

Kettle Crest South Trail

Snow Peak
7,103 ft.

O'Brien Creek

Snow Peak
Cabin

Snow Peak
Spring

COLVILLE
NATIONAL
FOREST

On the south side of Sherman Peak, the mountain hides any evidence of the highway, giving the area a wild and remote feeling. The trail remains fairly level, swelling between 6,100 and 6,400 feet as it continues to contour around the mountain. The east side of the mountain yields a long, unobstructed view toward the South Fork Sherman Creek valley. To the south you can see Snow Peak, Barnaby Buttes, and White Mountain, which the Kettle Crest South Trail weaves through.

After crossing a pass between Sherman Peak and a minor high point to the east, you'll switchback into a wide bowl on the mountain's east side. This is one of the most heavily burned sections of the hike. Next the trail crosses a ridge onto the north side of the peak below a cliff band high on the mountain. Talus extends almost to the trail in the final section before the path links up with the trail back to the parking lot.

Rather than climbing off-trail to Sherman Peak's summit, a better way to extend the trip is to walk an extra 1.4 miles south on the Kettle Crest South Trail to the Snow Peak Cabin, which sits in a beautiful and remote saddle between Snow Peak and Bald Mountain.

Miles and Directions

0.0 Start on the Kettle Crest South Trail 13. The trail dips into a drainage and back up toward US 20.

0.4 Cross US 20. Look for the trail just out of sight uphill, behind a boulder.

1.1 Turn right at a junction with Sherman Loop Trail 72. This is the beginning of the loop.

1.8 Pass through a burned area called Gleason's Gallop. Here there are many larches and views to the north.

3.1 Reach a junction with the Kettle Crest South Trail. Roam along this trail, or bear left to continue the loop.

5.0 Turn right onto the Kettle Crest South Trail and head back toward the parking lot, the end of the Sherman Loop Trail.

6.1 Arrive back at the trailhead.

Appendix A: Day Hike and Backpacking Checklist

Day Hike Checklist

- ❑ Collar, harness, bandanna, leash, permanent ID tag with home/cell number, and temporary tag
- ❑ Health and vaccination certificate
- ❑ Collapsible water bowl and water supply in metal or plastic bottle (32-ounce bottle for half-day hikes [under 4 hours]; 2-quart bottle for longer hikes). Eight ounces of water per dog per hour or 3.0 miles of hiking, in addition to water for you.
- ❑ Water purifier for full-day hike
- ❑ Kibble for your dog and snacks for you at mealtimes on the trail and extra protein snacks for energy boost for both. Save the yummiest treats for "recalls."
- ❑ Plastic resealable bags for carrying food, treats, medication, and first-aid essentials. The bags can be converted into food and water bowls as well as poop-scoop bags to carry waste out if necessary.
- ❑ Biodegradable poop-scoop bags
- ❑ Booties for pup; sturdy waterproof hiking footwear for you
- ❑ Dog packs (optional)
- ❑ Reflective vest for both you and your pup (if hiking during hunting season)
- ❑ Life vest for both you and your pup (if planning to be on water)
- ❑ Flyers for a lost dog
- ❑ Flea and tick application prior to hike
- ❑ Bug repellent in sealed plastic bag
- ❑ Sunscreen for you and your dog (tips of dog's ears)
- ❑ Sunhat and glasses for you
- ❑ Wire grooming brush to help remove stickers and foxtails from your dog's coat
- ❑ Extra clothing: sweater or coat for a thin-coated dog; breathable long-sleeved sweater and rain-repelling windbreaker for you
- ❑ Extra large, heavy-duty plastic garbage bags (good to sit on or to make a handy poncho in case of rain or to line the inside of your backpack)
- ❑ Pocketknife (Swiss Army–type knife that includes additional tools)
- ❑ Flashlight
- ❑ Matches or cigarette lighter and emergency fire starter
- ❑ Space blanket
- ❑ Whistle

- ❑ USGS maps, compass, GPS unit
- ❑ Extra batteries for electronic devices and flashlight
- ❑ Camera
- ❑ First-aid kit (phone numbers for National Animal Poison Control Center and your veterinarian)

Backpacking Checklist

Dog Necessities

- ❑ All items on day hike checklist, plus the following:
- ❑ Extra leash or rope
- ❑ Dog pack (optional)
- ❑ Doggie bedroll (foam sleeping pad)
- ❑ Dog's favorite chew toy
- ❑ Dog food (number of days on the trail × three meals a day)
- ❑ Additional water in a 2-quart bottle
- ❑ Dog snacks (enough for six rest stops per hiking day)
- ❑ Nylon tie-out line in camp (expandable leash can be extra leash and tie-out rope)

Human Necessities

- ❑ Tent with rain fly (large enough for you and your dog to sleep inside)
- ❑ Clothing (moisture-wicking socks, wind/rain gear, gloves, fleece or knit hat, long pants, wicking top, fleece top)
- ❑ Camp stove and fuel bottle
- ❑ Iodine tablets (backup water purifier)
- ❑ Food: lightweight, nutritious carbs and proteins—instant oatmeal, energy bars, granola, almond or peanut butter, dried fruits and nuts, dark chocolate for energy boosts, pasta, rice, canned tuna, dehydrated backpacking meals, tea bags or cocoa packets
- ❑ Extra garbage bags (use one in your backpack as a liner to keep contents dry in case of rain)
- ❑ Bear-proof food canisters
- ❑ Pepper spray (if hiking in bear country)

Note: Always let someone at home know where you are going and when you plan to return.

Appendix B: Trail Emergencies and First Aid

Using a Leash

Planning, a commonsense approach, and a leash will help prevent most mishaps on the trail. Keep your dog on leash when:

- Hiking in territory known for its higher concentration of specific hazards (bears, mountain lions, snakes, skunks)
- Crossing fast-moving streams
- Negotiating narrow mountainside trails
- Hiking in wind and snow (Dogs can become disoriented and lose their way.)

First Aid

If your dog gets into trouble, here are some basic first-aid treatments you can administer until you can get him to a vet.

Bleeding from Cuts or Wounds

1. Remove any obvious foreign object.
2. Rinse the area with warm water or 3 percent hydrogen peroxide.
3. Cover the wound with clean gauze or cloth, and apply firm, direct pressure over the wound for about 10 minutes to allow clotting to occur and bleeding to stop.
4. Place a nonstick pad or gauze over the wound and bandage with gauze wraps (the stretchy, clingy type). For a paw wound, cover the bandaging with a bootie. (An old sock with duct tape on the bottom is a good bootie substitute. Use adhesive tape around the sock to prevent it from slipping off. Be careful not to strangle circulation.)

Cardiopulmonary Resuscitation
Check with your veterinarian or local humane society for pet CPR classes.

Frostbite
Frostbite is the freezing of a body part exposed to extreme cold. Tips of ears and pads are the most vulnerable.

1. Remove your dog from the cold.
2. Apply a warm compress to the affected area without friction or pressure.

Heatstroke

Heatstroke occurs when a dog's body temperature is rising rapidly above 104°F and panting is ineffective to regulate temperature.

1. Get your dog out of the sun and begin reducing body temperature (no lower than 103°F) by applying water-soaked towels on her head (to cool the brain), chest, abdomen, and feet.
2. Let your dog stand in a pond, lake, or stream while you gently pour water on her. Avoid icy water—it can chill her. Swabbing the footpads with alcohol will help.

Hypothermia

Hypothermia occurs when a dog's body temperature drops below 95°F because of overexposure to cold weather.

1. Take the dog indoors or into a sheltered area where you can make a fire.
2. Wrap him in a blanket, towel, sleeping bag, your clothing, or whatever you have available.
3. Wrap him in warm towels or place warm water bottles in a towel next to him.
4. Hold him close to you for body heat.

Insect Bites

Bee stings and spider bites may cause itching, swelling, and hives. If the stinger is still present, scrape it off with your nail or tweezers at the base away from the point of entry. (Pressing the stinger or trying to pick it from the top can release more toxin.) Apply a cold compress to the area and spray it with a topical analgesic like Benadryl spray to relieve the itch and pain. As a precaution, carry an over-the-counter antihistamine (such as Benadryl) and ask your vet about the appropriate dosage before you leave, in case your dog has an extreme allergic reaction with excessive swelling.

Getting Skunked

When your dog gets skunked, a potent, smelly cloud of spray burns his eyes and makes his mouth foam. The smell can make you gag, and contact with the spray on your dog's coat can give your skin a tingling, burning sensation. Apply de-skunking shampoo as soon as possible.

De-Skunking Shampoo Mix

1 quart hydrogen peroxide
¼ cup baking soda
1 tablespoon dishwashing detergent

Put on rubber gloves and thoroughly wet your dog; apply mixture and let stand for 15 minutes. Rinse and repeat as needed.

Sore Muscles

1. Rest your dog.

2. Apply cold-water compresses to tight muscle areas to reduce inflammation.

3. Administer Ascriptin (buffered aspirin). Check with your vet on dosage for your dog's breed and weight.

Venomous Bites

1. Keep your dog calm (activity stimulates the absorption of venom).

2. Rinse the area with water, and transport your dog to the nearest vet.

First-Aid Kit Checklist

- ❑ First-aid book, such as *Field Guide: Dog First Aid Emergency Care of the Outdoor Dog* by Randy Acker, DVM.

- ❑ Muzzle; even the most loving dogs can snap and bite when in pain. Muzzles come in different styles and sizes to fit all dog nose shapes.

- ❑ Ascriptin (buffered aspirin); older dogs in particular may be stiff and sore at the end of a hike or backpacking excursion. Consult your vet on the appropriate dosage.

- ❑ Antidiarrheal agents and gastrointestinal protectants; Pepto-Bismol—1 to 3 ml/kg/day, Kaopectate—1 to 2 ml/kg every 2–6 hours

- ❑ Indigestion and stomach upset. Pepcid (famotidine) decreases gastric acid secretions. Try a dosage of 0.1 to 2 mg/kg every 12–24 hours.

- ❑ Scissors (with rounded tips) for trimming hair around a wound

- ❑ Hydrogen peroxide (3 percent) to disinfect surface abrasions and wounds

- ❑ Antiseptic ointment

- ❑ Gauze pads and gauze

- ❑ Clingy and elastic bandages

- ❑ Sock or bootie to protect a wounded foot

- ❑ Duct tape to wrap around the sole of a sock used as a bootie

- ❑ Tweezers to remove ticks, needles, or foreign objects in a wound

- ❑ Hemostats

- ❑ Styptic powder for bleeding

- ❑ Rectal thermometer

- ❑ Hydrocortisone spray to relieve plant rashes and stings

- ❑ Lemon juice for quick rinse (recipe for de-skunking shampoo mix)

- ❑ Your veterinarian's telephone number and the ASPCA National Animal Poison Control Center (888-426-4435) taped inside the kit

Appendix C: Wildlife Conflicts

On the trail, you and your dog are in someone else's home. Be the kind of guest you would want in your house. Be considerate of those who live there, disturb nothing as you pass through, and take only the memory of the experience and photographs of the beauty that moved you.

Protecting Wildlife and Your Dog

The surest way to avoid wildlife conflicts is to keep your dog on a leash. Dogs chasing deer deplete the wild animal of its survival energy and can cause debilitating injury to both the pursued and the pursuer.

Curious dogs nosing around off leash risk incurring the pungent wrath of a skunk, the painful quills of a porcupine, or a bite from an ill-tempered rattlesnake. All are responding defensively to a perceived threat and are not lurking to attack you or your dog.

Birds nesting in meadows and low brush are vulnerable to roaming dogs in spring, and fawns can fall prey to your dog's primal instincts. These animals are not hosting you and your dog in their home by choice, so be respectful guests.

Some trails cross cattle- and sheep-grazing land. Keep in mind that a dog harassing stock can be shot.

Keep your dog on leash for the first 30 minutes of a hike to give her a chance to absorb some of the new sights, smells, and sounds that might make her lose control with excitement fresh out of the gate and make her more likely to burn off excess energy chasing wildlife or trying to entice cattle to a game of tag.

Preventing Encounters

With regard to predators, the potential for being attacked by a wild animal in Washington is extremely low compared to many other natural hazards. Wildlife sightings are a privilege. Wolves, bears, and mountain lions, when given the option, generally prefer avoidance over confrontation with humans unless you are a threat to them or their young.

Coyotes and bobcats are just as elusive and usually find rodents satisfying enough. But small dogs could be considered tender morsels and should be kept on leash especially at dawn and dusk, when predators are most likely to search for food.

Development and human intrusion are at the core of encounter problems. Encroachment on habitat and more hikers in the backcountry have exposed bears and coyotes to human food and garbage. Animals accustomed to easy meals become brazen and can pose a threat to human safety. Sadly, humans create these "problem" animals. Destruction, not relocation, is usually their fate. There's a good reason for the "Don't feed wildlife" campaign.

This is not to say that a dog responsive to voice control should not enjoy tagging along and bounding with joy off leash, but be informed about the area where you plan to hike, and when in doubt make your presence known with a small bell attached to your pack, dog harness, or walking stick. Stay on the trail, and talk or hum to avoid surprising a bear in the berry bushes or startling a big cat from his nap.

Bear Safety

In bear country, when it comes to odor, the motto is "Less is safer." Pack all food items (human and dog) and any other odorous items in airtight resealable bags. Dispose of all items with food smells in airtight bags and place in bear-proof storage containers. Clean your dishes and pet bowls as quickly as possible so that food smells do not float through the forest as a dinner invitation to the local bears. Some national forests and wilderness areas require campers to use plastic portable "bear-resistant food canisters." These canisters (some collapsible) are available for sale and rent at sporting goods stores and some ranger stations.

If you see a bear in the distance, stop, stay calm, and don't run. Keep your dog close to your side on leash. You should feel awe rather than panic. Walk a wide upwind detour so the animal can get your scent, and make loud banging or clanging noises as you leave the area. If the bear is at closer range, the same principles apply while you keep your eye on the bear and back down the trail slowly if the terrain doesn't allow you to negotiate a detour.

Avoid sudden movements that could spook or provoke the bear. Be cool, slow, but deliberate as you make your retreat.

Bears and wild animals in general prefer anonymity. If they know you are out there, they will avoid your path.

BEAR FACTS

- Bears can run, swim, and climb trees.
- Bears have good vision, excellent hearing, and a superior sense of smell.
- Bears are curious and attracted to food smells.
- Bears can be out at any time of day but are most active in the coolness of dawn and dusk and after dark.

Mountain Lions

There are fewer mountain lions than bears in Washington. Here are some tips.

Keep your dog on leash on the trail.

Keep your dog in the tent at night.

Seeing doesn't mean attacking. If you come across a mountain lion, stay far enough away to give it the opportunity to avoid you. Do not approach or provoke the lion. Instead, walk away slowly and maintain eye contact. Running will stimulate the lion's predatory instinct to chase and hunt. Make yourself big by putting your arms above your head and waving them. Use your jacket or walking stick above your head to appear bigger. Do not bend down or make any motion that will make you look or sound like easy prey. Shout and make noise. If necessary, walking sticks can be weapons, as can rocks or anything you can get your hands on to fight back with.

For more information on hiking in mountain lion country, refer to *Mountain Lion Alert* by Steven Torres (Falcon Publishing, 1997).

MOUNTAIN LION FACTS

Mountain lions are elusive, and preying on humans is uncharacteristic. Mountain lions are most active at dawn and dusk and usually hunt at night. They are solitary and secretive and require a vegetated habitat for camouflage while they stalk prey. Their meal of choice is big game (deer, bighorn sheep, and elk). In the absence of game, however, they can make a meal of domestic livestock and small mammals. They feed on what they kill. An unattended dog in camp is far more appetizing than his kibble.

Snakes

Most dogs have an instinctive aversion to anything that slithers and will jump away at first sight, sound, or touch. Snakebites are usually the result of stepping on a snake unknowingly rather than conscious provocation. Most snakebites occur on the nose or front legs and can be lethal to a small or young dog. If taken to the vet quickly, larger adult dogs will survive the majority of bites. Ask your veterinarian if the recently developed rattlesnake vaccine would benefit your dog. Ask your vet or local dog club about snake avoidance classes in your area. (See Appendix B for treatment of venomous bites.)

Appendix D: Sources for Pooch Gear and Useful Websites

bringfido.com: help with locating dog-friendly lodging

natgeomaps.com: a source for trail maps

recreation.gov: public land campground reservations

rei.com: outdoor recreation gear cooperative with stores throughout Washington. You can shop for Fido's hiking gear, accessories, and dog-friendly hiking guide books.

reserveamerica.com: online camping reservations

ruffwear.com: online source for outdoor gear and accessories for dogs

store.usgs.gov: purchase of USGS maps

wilderness.net: online source for purchasing topographic maps and links to wilderness information

wolfpacks.com: custom dog packs

wta.org: The Washington Trail Association website has tons of hiking information as well as some specific information on dog-friendly hikes.

youdidwhatwithyourweiner.com: useful information about hiking with dogs in Washington, and entertaining tales to boot

Hike Index